Investing Megatr

MW01234309

Beginners Guide to Earning Lifetime Passive Income with Small, Safe Investments in Marijuana Stocks, CBD, REITs, Gold and Cryptocurrency

Written By

Everyman Investing

Contents

Introduction 5

Chapter 1: Investing Basics 6

Chapter 2: Investment Essentials...14

Chapter 3: Financial Management – and how to ensure you get the most for your money........ 24

Chapter 4: Cultivating a Profitable Investing Mindset 27

Chapter 5: Fundamental vs. Technical analysis of stocks – which is more effective for the novice investor?... 33

Chapter 6: An Introduction to Dividends – The Lifeblood of Any Investor 40

Chapter 7: Diversification and Risk Management 50

Chapter 8: How to Profitably Select Individual Stocks...................... 62

Conclusion – The 7 Golden Investment Rules for Long-Term Profitability and Life-Long Financial Prosperity..73

Introduction 76

Chapter One: Growth Stocks...77

Chapter Two Value Stocks 95

Chapter Three Growth Portfolio Allocations 103

Chapter Four Growth Stocks Part 1 117

Chapter Five Growth Stocks Part 2...132

Chapter Six Growth Stocks Part 3...145

Chapter Seven Growth Stocks Part 4...156

Conclusion 168

Stock Investing for Beginners

The 7 Golden Investment Rules & Strategies for Passive Income and Lifetime Wealth Building with Value Investing

By

Everyman Investing

Introduction

Success in life comes from, more than anything else, financial freedom. Financial freedom means that you can always satisfy your human needs without much struggle. It involves building wealth to insulate yourself from possible future loss of productivity, be it voluntary or involuntary.

In short, the money you make when you are actively involved in money-making activities, like your job, should cover your needs past retirement without you having to forego any of the comforts you are accustomed to.

But that money is often not enough on its own. You need to invest it and make your money become a second job for you, generating great profit for you over time to make you richer than you could ever dream. The stock market is one of the most profitable investment areas for people intending to create wealth over a long time. Contrary to what you may have heard, one of the safest investments you can make is to start a stock portfolio. If you do your homework well enough, there will be little chance of you losing your investment. This isn't my opinion, this if factual based on hundreds of years of data.

It is not even complicated. Anyone can be successful in the stock market if they do their research, distance themselves from "insider tips" or noise, and are patient. While the stock market is definitely not a get-rich-quick kind of investment. Your investment portfolio works like your bank account, but with one major difference. If you make the right selections and invest right, it is near guaranteed to make you a lot of money in the long run.

In additional to this, every person already has an insider advantage for investing based on the area they work in. For example, a dentist may notice that a certain brand of floss works much better and is much more prevalent than competing brands. Familiarity is a very important aspect of creating a stock portfolio. Invest in a company whose future you believe to be strong and you never have to worry about losing money.

Chapter 1: Investing Basics

Why invest at all?

Most financial advisors encourage people to focus on saving first before thinking about investing. The logic behind that reasoning is that savings are "safer" than investments, making it harder to lose money. The internet is chock-full with these "experts." And while they are well-meaning people who only want to help you maintain your current financial situation, a little more aggressive money-management strategy is needed if upward mobility is your financial aim.

You see, the overall effect of the "save first and invest much later" approach is to make you overemphasize the benefits of savings- and there are quite a few of these- at the expense of the greater profit of investing. Investing is not something for you to fear. Nor is it the last thing you should do after saving a year's worth of your monthly expenses. If you do it the right way, investing can become a legitimate way for you to save money at higher interest rates than a bank would ever give you.

The most compelling reason given for the need to put money in a savings account is emergency expenditure. This is a valid reason, but the thing to realize is that money you put in your bank account in savings ends up being money you put lying around waiting for possible emergency expenditures. The bank then takes your money and invests it in real estate, bonds, the stock market, and trust funds, makes a bunch of money, and gives you a tiny fraction of this money as incentive for you to save more. The bottom-line is this; your savings make someone rich, but that someone is <u>not you</u>.

It is not that you should not save. You will actually have to accumulate some savings before taking the leap and investing your money for higher returns. The aim of this book is to show you that you need to remove the emphasis on savings and think more about investing because that is where the real money will be made.

Think of it this way; your savings account is simply a tank where you store a portion of your yearly earnings but your investment portfolio is another job that brings in money from the money made in your 9-5. In essence, a well-executed investment portfolio is a second job that sends more money to your savings account, money which you can re-invest for greater rewards. If you follow the lessons contained in this book, you should learn how to invest in the stock market at little to no risk. And with the ease of electronic share trading and transfer of money from stockbroker accounts, liquidity should not be an issue either.

The Federal Reserve no longer sets bank interests at rates higher than the level of inflation. As such, most banks give you a 1% rate on savings, which adds negligible money to your account. In fact, when you factor in the inflation rates, a savings account takes purchasing power out of your pocket at just a slightly higher rate than keeping your money buried in your backyard as a savings plan.

Generally, the only advantage that putting your money in a savings account has over investing is that you can access your money much faster from a savings account, especially if your investment happens to be an asset that you will have to liquidate. However, with the stock market, the issue of liquidity becomes less of an issue. If the need arises, you can sell your shares easily through an app and receive your money in two or three days. Exactly the time you will need to move money from a savings account to a drawing account!

Now if getting your hands on money from a stock portfolio takes roughly the same time as withdrawing from a savings account and investing in stocks generates much higher returns, why does everyone advise you to focus on saving? The answer is very simple: risk. Every investment has its risks and a stock portfolio is no different. The stock market tends to be volatile from time to time so there is a chance that you might lose money.

But the returns and potential for making good money far exceeds that of suffering a loss. And if you do your homework well and choose the right companies to invest in, this risk will be reduced greatly. This book will introduce you to the 7Golden Rules of investing that will teach you to invest prudently and help you minimize the risk of losing money on the stock market.

The alternative is to put your money in a savings account and have inflation gradually erode it over time. Inflation is a simple enough phenomenon of free market economies that happens as a result of increased supply of money in a country and increasing cost of raw material for producing commodities, leading higher commodity prices. This in turn causes the price of commodities to rise year after year, meaning that you need more money to buy any given commodities today than you needed, say, five years ago.

What does inflation mean to your savings? The purchasing power of a dollar decreases over time, so $1,000 saved today will give you far less value in one year's time. And even though your principal earns some interest, banks rarely give enough interest to replace the purchasing power your principal loses to inflation every year. Inflation has such an adverse effect on your savings because banks rarely offer interest rates that are high enough to replace the purchasing power you lose to rising prices of commodities in the open market.

Taking the $1,000 given above, if your bank gives you a 1% interest rate p.a. (which is what most banks give), your money will have gained $10 at the end of that one year. Most people look at the interest rate and think, "well, it is money I wouldn't have made if I had spent it all, so that's okay." The inflation runs at about 2-4% in a stable economy. To take the lowest figure, let's assume that the rate of inflation was 2% in the year you saved $1,000. That translates to a $20 loss in purchasing power. So in actuality, your savings plan just took $10 out of your pocket. When the rate of inflation is higher, you lose more money from your savings account.

To put inflation in perspective, the average price of a movie ticket rose 42.5% between 2005 and 2018 from $6.41 to $9.14. The overall inflation in the 20-year period between 1999 and 2018 was 50.7%, meaning that you would need $1,507 in 2018 to buy a commodity priced at $1,000 in 1999. For the same time period, $1000 saved in a bank that gives a 1% compound interest would have accumulated just $221. With simple interest, the accumulated amount would be $200. That means that if you save $1,000 in a bank, you are looking at about $286 reduction in purchasing power.

Now let's look at the alternative in investment. If you had put the $1,000 in a stock portfolio and bought shares whose price rose 7% over one year (which, in most cases, is a modest figure) then you just added $70 to your investment. In twenty years, the $1,000 investment would have grown to $4,309. Take out the $507 lost to inflation and your $1,000 has just made you a very respectable $2,802 in passive income. If you decide to pump $100 every year into your investment portfolio, then you will have accumulated about $8,257 in the 20 years. In contrast, pumping the same amount into the savings account will generate just $3,445 in the same time period. Adjusted for inflation, the figure for investment seems even more respectable.

Investing vs. Trading – What's The Difference?

Investing and trading are two very different terms that both relate to transacting in the stock market. A lot of people use the two terms interchangeably, but they could not be more distinct. It is completely wrong to refer to trading as investing, just as it is wrong to say that you are trading when you are actually investing.

Trading is defined as a stock purchase that is made with the intention to sell in a short time when the price goes up. Serious traders spend countless hours gathering intelligence on companies that are listed on the stock market. With the idea being to buy when the price is low and sell after a spike, you will need to be much attuned to the goings-on behind the scenes to be half sure that a trade will make you money. Even then, such transactions are simply speculative in nature and you can never be sure of making money.

In fact, trading bears more resemblance to gambling than to business because you buy based on a "hunch" you may have that something may happen to favor you, but you have no control whatsoever on the outcome. You may have seen the upbeat YouTube ads promoting "trading" apps that allow you to bet, in real time, on the direction of a stock's price. To be a trader, you will have to become very good at reading charts and predicting possible rise in prices of stocks in the short term. It is a rather cumbersome and unproductive approach to building wealth. You are better off steering clear of trading and focusing on longer term transactions with a more productive return. You are better off investing.

Investing, on the other hand, entails a more dedicated scrutiny of a company to determine its long term prospects over a period of up to twenty years. Investors study a company's financial ratios, business model, leadership, competition, and growth strategy and if the company turns out to be strong enough, proceed to invest their hard-earned money in its future. The trend of stocks for good companies is always in an upwards trajectory, which means that the risk of losing money is very small. The preliminary research also serves as an ironclad assurance to the investor that their intention to invest in a company is the right thing to do.

Moreover, investing in a company's long term future entitles you to dividends that you can re-invest and boosts your stake for more profits. Dividends are not available to traders. The transaction fees that investors pay to buy and sell stock are also less because their transactions are few. Traders are charged every time they make a transaction and with trading being a volume transactions endeavor, they end up paying quite a lot of money. If trading is the speculation in the short term price fluctuations of a stock, investing is the iron-clad belief in a company's profitability in the long run.

To make money as an investor, you will want to make your initial choice good enough so that you can hold on to the stock even when the price dips from time to time. The thing to realize is that these dips are to be expected and that no stock ever maintains its price at a constant or climbs steadily. You will need the discipline to stop yourself from selling at the first sign of danger, otherwise you may keep selling and buying like a trader and that will most probably lose some of your money in the process.

In your quest for success in stock investment, you should look up to some of the industry's best investors like Warren Buffett. In a career spanning decades, Warren Buffett has invested in a handful of very profitable companies and grown his personal finances to over $70 billion, becoming one of the world's wealthiest men. His advice to investors is to close the doors and not follow the market. According to Buffett, going against the current on a business you believe in will always be more profitable than following the market on a company whose operations you don't have a clue about.

On the other hand, stock trading guru George Soros advises potential traders to bet on the unexpected. With a net worth of about $25 billion, Soros has engaged in countless trades over several decades; nearly the same amount of time Buffett has been investing.

The fortunes amassed by these two men demonstrate better than anything the differences between investing and trading. It also shows that real money is to be made from investing, not trading. To engage in stock trading you have to be ready to lose money from time to time just like in gambling. To invest in stocks you have to be prepared for the monotony that follows an investment. Investment guru Paul Samuelson best captions the difference between trading and investing by comparing one to Las Vegas and the other to watching paint dry.

Why you should avoid Day Trading

You might have heard of certain people getting rich from so-called day trading. Well, if stock trading is speculative, it has got nothing on day trading. Stock traders may buy a stock and hold on to it for a few weeks or months while they await its price to climb, but day traders have to buy on the same day. For big bourses like the New York Stock Exchange, this means that day trading has to happen within six and a half hours. There is simply no way to make the buy and sell decision other than blind speculation.

And while you may pick out a couple of winners and make a lot of money with those couple lucky breaks, the odds are that you will lose ghastly amounts doing this kind of financial speculation. There is nothing to day trading but blind guesswork. In fact, the practice bears greater resemblance to betting than business. As long as your aim for engaging in the stock market remains to be profit-making, you should keep off day trading at all costs. Instead, you should engage in more profitable undertakings like value investing.

How do guys like Warren Buffett make so much money in the stock market?

To understand why wizards of Wall Street like Warren Buffett are so wealth. We must first understand value investing. To understand value investing, you will need to be conversant with the basic workings of the stock market. The simplest fact to understand about stocks is that they represent the value the public places on a company. By multiplying the price of a company's share with the number of shares in the market, you will find its market valuation. By digging a little deeper into the company's financial documents –like its balance sheet- you will find its actual worth, called book value. If a company's market capitalization is lower than its book value, then that is a buying opportunity because by the principle of market equilibrium, the stock price will rise to match its intrinsic value.

Value investing is the equivalent of buying dollar bills for 90 cents because you are guaranteed to make money once the rest of the market discovers the true value of the company. There are few companies whose market valuation is lower than their intrinsic value, but if you can find them, then you should target them and hold on to them. Targeting stocks which you believe are undervalued relative to their long term health is a strategy used by investment gurus like Warren Buffett.

To find stocks that have the potential for the best earnings, you will need to be familiar with the price/earnings (P/E) financial ratios and price-to-book ratios. The idea is to find companies whose share prices are almost guaranteed to rise.

Comparing the price of a company's shares to its earnings will help you weed out shares that have been inflated by market hype. Low P/E ratios indicate less discrepancy between a company's stocks and its true financial status. After finding a company with a low P/E ratio, further research will be needed to determine that the stock is not simply bad and likely to lose even more value.

Price-to-book ratios also indicate the discrepancy between what the company thinks a company is worth and its true value. Rarely will you find a company with a 1:1 ratio and rarer even to find a P/B ratio where the price is lower than the book value. But these are the most lucrative stocks, so you should look out for them. Another reason to do value investing is when a company offers exceptionally high dividend yields. High dividend yields indicate that the financial health of a company is good, but it could simply mean that the company just wants to attract investors, so be careful with that. A failsafe way to do it is to look at all three but keep in mind that only the calculations you can do for yourself; the P/B and P/E ratios can really give you an accurate idea of a stock's attractiveness.

You may be wondering why everyone wouldn't be buying undervalued stocks if value investing is like buying 90 cents for $1. Well, value investing is made possible by one very simple fact; the market overreacts to bad news. When the market finds out that a company is facing difficulties, getting investigated, or the quarterly earnings do not match projections, many people opt to sell. The laws of supply and demand come into play, meaning that the prices drop, often below the company's book value.

This is a buying opportunity for smart investors. If you are planning to buy a company's shares and you are confident about its long-term financial health, buying when everyone is selling at lower prices is the best idea. If you own stocks and some bad news do not make you doubt the overall financial health of your vested company, buy more. The price will ultimately rise to the old levels and probably climb higher. Warren Buffett, Peter Lynch, and other investors have been doing it since they started their investment career and they are doing great.

A perfect example of a great value investment opportunity is the November 2016 Fitbit fiasco. After releasing third quarter earnings that were lower than the market expected, the company lost 19% of its value in a single day as investors rushed to rid themselves of the stock. A year later, earnings were up 50% and its shares had soared again. However, the only reason Fitbit had reported lower profits in the 2016 Q3 was because it had invested heavily in research and development. Otherwise its financials remained strong, even bullish. That meant that investors were losing confidence in the company for the wrong reasons. Buying such a stock at its lowest would be doubly advantageous because after the R&D that had caused the lower earnings figures, would come products that would send its sales soaring and share price shooting too. A higher share price would be all but guaranteed.

These types of cases are many. To be a smart investor, you have to go beyond what is seen by everyone in the market and look at the long term prospects before buying or selling. In the following chapters of this book, you will find more details on how to cushion your investment from the turbulence of arbitrary price drops and rises and, when the opportunity arises with minimal risk to your money, buy when others are selling.

By the same rule of value investing, you should have a price ceiling past which you can be fairly certain that the price of a stock you currently hold cannot go higher. This should be in those instances where the market has driven the price so high that the P/E and P/B ratios indicate a guaranteed price decline. Sometimes the price shoots to levels way above what is logical for a stock. At this point, you sell because there is an opportunity to make good money and maybe invest in another company, or hold the money and buy more shares when the price comes back to normal levels.

Sometimes a company's share price just climbs and climbs. For example, Apple went public in 1980 with an initial share price of $22. But leadership disputes forced Steve Jobs out and the company faltered, with the price reaching lows of as little as $14 in 2002. The company currently trades at almost $200, a huge gain on capital. Moreover, the shares have undergone several splits so that one share in 2002 has been split into 56 in 2019.

A $1,000 investment in Apple shares in 2002 would be worth about $110,000 as of April 12, 2019. The share price has fluctuated over the years, but the amazing 110-fold increase in investment proves that if you believe in the future prospects of a company, then you should hold on to the stock regardless of short-term indications.

The flipside of this is that sometimes the market is just a little more excited about the future prospects of a company and the company experiences explosive growth with the price reaching anticipated levels. Many startup tech companies have experienced such growth 3-5 years after their IPOs. Such spikes in prices are normal, even expected, for younger companies. It is the older, more mature companies that should warrant selling when prices go beyond a certain price.

By looking at the financial ratios introduced later in the book, you will be able to determine at what levels it would make more sense to cash out on your momentarily overpriced stock. This does not make you a trader, it makes you a smart investor because you are able to recognize a selling opportunity and act on it. You should not do this when you are starting out or if you have not already identified another good stock to invest in.

Chapter 2: Investment Essentials

In chapter 1, you read how investing is better than saving as far as building your wealth is concerned. You also got to read how inflation reduces the value of your savings by eroding your purchasing power. You were also introduced to the concept of value investing through which it will be possible for you to purchase undervalued quality stocks and sell them at a higher price for assured profits. In this chapter, you will learn the minute details of investing as your training in expert (or at least well informed) investment advances. The first thing you will need to learn is managing your funds.

Best Brokerage Accounts for New Investors

A brokerage account is your ticket to the world of stock investment. Like a bank account, it allows you to deposit funds and with these funds, transact in the stock market. The only place to open a brokerage account is in a brokerage firm, either online or in a brick-and-mortar branch. Opening a brokerage account is as easy as opening a bank account or, in the case of online brokerage accounts, registering for any online service. All you need is your social security number, the name and address of your employer where applicable, and the details of the bank account you will use to inject money into your brokerage account.

There are numerous types of brokerage accounts that you can open, just as there are more than a dozen brokerage firms in which to do it. The broker is the most important aspect of the stock trading operation and without a broker you cannot transact. So choose your broker very, very carefully. You should do your research before making your decision. Be thorough. Talk to your broker. Ask questions. Find out what people are saying about them in online forums.

Your broker will be a critical aspect of your investment plan and you simply cannot afford to make a mistake. I will introduce a few brokers late in this section, but it is upon you to ensure that whomever you choose is the right firm to entrust your investment plan. First, you need to learn a few pertinent issues pertaining to brokerage accounts.

Brokers make money from the stock market through transactions made by investors and traders alike. They make money from a commission charge on every buy or sell transaction, usually about $7. If you don't want to execute the buy/sell orders yourself, you can pay an advisory fee to your broker for him to do them for you. While you will make the decision to buy or sell, some brokerage packages allow you to give automatic buy/sell orders when the price reaches certain levels. Finally, you need to keep in mind that brokerage firms do not necessarily allow all types of investments. This should be part of your preliminary research before settling for a broker to open an account with.

Now that you know the basics of a brokerage account, you should know the different types of accounts that exist and the options they present to you. Online brokerage accounts are web-based accounts that give you the opportunity to transact over the internet. Brokerage firms have created mobile and computer applications and trading portals from which you can transact in the comfort of your living room, the subway, or even in the office.

Online accounts have the huge advantage of giving you great power to transact at any time from any place. You can simply activate notifications and receive real-time updates, allowing you to keep a close eye on the goings-on on Wall Street as far as your stock goes. With the volatility of the stock market, those value investing opportunities may only come but once and if you are not there to capitalize, you will lose a great investment. And while you will not be engaging in short-term transactions like a trader, you will need a diversified stock portfolio, so picking up as many undervalued stocks as you can find will be good for you. We will go into more details about diversification later in the book.

Another type of brokerage account is the managed or full-service account. With full-service accounts, you get the added advantage of a dedicated advisor, human or artificially engineered, to guide you through your investment journey. This type of account also has the added advantage of easing your labors in managing your portfolio by allowing you to set investment goals. For example, if you want to buy company X shares but want to buy them at prices below a certain value under a set of conditions and you don't have the time or resources to keep an eye on the market, you can entrust these details with your managed account liaison and they will handle these transactions for you.

The last type of account is the retirement option where you put your Individual Retirement Account (IRA) funds into a brokerage account. These accounts are stricter on cash withdrawals, restricting your when and how, often into the distant future. A main advantage of retirement accounts is that they receive better tax breaks, with your capital gains being spared the taxation year-on-year until you are ready to withdraw after retirement. Taxes on share earnings reduce the capital gains for other types of brokerage accounts quite substantially. With retirement investment accounts, you should not forget to furnish the broker with details of a next of kin who take over the account when you are no longer around to run it.

Now that you know the different options that are available for you, let us run through the brokerage firms with whom you can create accounts. There are numerous such brokers, but we will touch on six of the best, namely; Charles Schwab, Vanguard, Fidelity, TD Ameritrade, E-Trade, and Robinhood. Out of these, you will get a clear enough picture of the options available for you out there. And while these brokers come highly recommended, you are encouraged to vet each one extensively before opening an account with them.

Charles Schwab

Charles Schwab is a comprehensive brokerage firm that provides you with a range of stock trading services. The firm has adopted technological advances in the stock market like online trading to enable account-holders to transact online. Charles Schwab is also dedicated to offering guidance to beginner investors through services such as StreetSmart Edge, an array of native mobile apps, and a satisfaction guarantee system.

Charles Schwab offers a user-friendly trading experience through the StreetSmart website, mobile and desktop applications, and cloud services. The sites offer real-time news and research from reputable analysts and financial repertoire like MarketEdge, Reuters, and Credit Suisse among others. You can perform a comprehensive analysis on your stock using the news and research features provided within the site before transacting.

Charles Schwab charges relatively small commission fees for transactions on its platforms. For every stock or ETF trade, you will be charged the rock-bottom price of $4.95 (the lowest of all brokers reviewed in this book). Schwab ETTs attract $0 commission, and options attract a $4.95, with each contract being charged $0.65. You will not be required to maintain a minimum balance with Schwab either.

And while Schwab seems to cater more to traders than investors with its share price live stream and automatic functions, it offers a wide range of options for stocks, ETFs (discussed later in this book), international indexes, and funds. The firm also has an online bank -the Charles Schwab Bank- that allows Schwab users to move money easily from their brokerage account to their bank accounts. You may use your Schwab Bank Visa card anywhere in the world with no extra charges.

Vanguard

Vanguard is the ultimate long-term investment brokerage firm. The firm is set up as a not-for-profit institution with its funds being the legitimate owners of the company. The firm is particularly well positioned for investments in ETFs and mutual funds with over 1,800 commission-free ETFs and a huge selection of low-cost funds. With a $3,000 minimum in deposit fees and $7 charge per ETF and stock trade and $7 for options and $1 for every contract, the firm's business model favors buy-and-hold investors.

Vanguard's online support is also woefully lacking. The website requires you to refresh to bring up the latest stock prices, which might lead to a trader missing out on a wonderful buying or selling opportunity. That should not necessarily be a problem for you as a prospective investor. However, the fact that there is no online chat feature on its platforms or that you cannot buy or sell stocks online is rather disappointing. To receive robo-advisory services on Vanguard, you are going to need a minimum of $5,000 in your account.

Overall, Vanguard is a good brokerage firm for long term investments, but with the minimal online support and trading features, you should have support stock trading means, like the NYSE or NASDAQ apps to trade on. Vanguard also demands higher account balances and investments than other brokers, but the plentiful supply of low-cost funds will probably make up for the shortfalls in trading support.

Fidelity

Fidelity Investments is one of the highest rated stock brokers, presenting its clients with a blend of tools and services. The firm has also been working to improve its online infrastructure after a crash-plagued 2018. Fidelity's online platform, Active Trader Pro, allows users to access live data on stock prices and reviews as well as providing an easy way to buy or sell your shares.

The charges are lower than Vanguard's but slightly higher than Schwab's, with stock and ETF trades attracting a $4.95 commission fee for each buy or sell order. Trading in options attract a similar charge, with contracts setting you back $0.65. Fidelity requires no account minimum. With excellent trade executions, detailed ETF studies, and low and easy-to-understand fees, Fidelity was ranked first in the 2019 list of best American stock brokers by Investopedia.

The company offers outstanding support for traders and investors alike. Fidelity's mobile apps allow you to add stocks to a watch list and monitor their progress before committing to an investment. Apart from online support features on its platforms, the firm allows account-holders to reach its service centers through Facebook, iMessage, Amazon Alexa, and Google Assistant. Robo- advisory services are also expected to be rolled out in the near future.

Much like Vanguard, Fidelity offers its customers with a wide variety of international stocks, indexes, and funds. Over 250 ETFs are offered at zero commission. Fidelity also offers its customers with a full range of banking capabilities, complete with Federal Deposit Insurance Corporation (FDIC) insurance for equities held through the firm's brokerage account. Apart from insuring your stocks from market volatility, Fidelity has one of the most comprehensive online education programs of any stock broker. Among the educational materials available for your perusal include videos, webinars, online coaching, and articles on a range of topics and issues. With Fidelity, you can also rest easy with the knowledge that your broker will always be working to improve their services to you.

TD Ameritrade

TD Ameritrade is the first discount brokerage firm reviewed in this list. A publicly traded company, TD Ameritrade is home to more than 10 million users, with more than 900,000 transactions taking place through the firm's platforms on any given day. TD offers one of the most comprehensive arrays of price comparison tools, complete with real-time stock prices and advanced analysis. These services are offered in the company's proprietary analysis tool known as thinkorswim and it incorporates advanced prediction algorithms, including corporate calendars, in its analysis. Because of thinkorswim, Ameritrade ranks highly on trading platforms and ease of use.

You can also expect to receive the best in investment training through TD Ameritrade Network, a live streaming financial channel that provides you with amazing market analysis from expert investors. TD Ameritrade also offers daily commentary through a wide range of publications like The Ticker Tape, thinkMoney, and a TD Ameritrade digital magazine published on a quarterly basis.

On pricing, TD Ameritrade has always been one of the most expensive brokers in the market until recently when it slashed its commission fees to compete with the likes of Schwab, Vanguard, and Fidelity. While every trade attracted a $9.99 commission two years ago, the company now charges $6.95, just a few cents below Vanguard. The commission obviously straddles the thin line between mass appeal and premium charges for the premium services the company offers.

As for the trading versus investing bend in their services, TD Ameritrade seems to lean more towards investing than trading. They offer customers with more than 4,000 commission-free mutual funds and over 300 commission-free ETFs. A rather exorbitant commission of $13.90

for any ETF you sell less than 30 days after buying encourages longer-term ETF holding. However, Ameritrade is limited in the international division, providing customers with only US and Canadian stocks.

Deposits on Ameritrade are also uninsurable with the FDIC, although you can count on ATM fee reimbursement, online payment services, and mobile check deposit. So, even though TD Ameritrade is an excellent broker with cutting-edge technological services and superior user experience on its platforms, you will be somewhat limited in the types of stocks you can invest in (only America and Canada). If you don't plan to invest in foreign-listed companies out of USA and Canada, then TD Ameritrade will more than fit the bill. However, if you plan to invest in emerging markets (we will talk about them later in the book) or foreign-based international indexes, this may not be a very good option for you.

E-Trade

E-Trade is an exclusively online stockbroker that serves millions of customers through its ETrade.com flagship website and a host of mobile applications. The standard commission charged on E-Trade transactions is $6.95 on every stock and ETF transaction. High volume traders, more than 30 transactions in the last three months and accountholders with over $250,000 in their accounts, qualify for a lower commission of $4.95.A minimum balance of $500 is also required for E-Trade. Evidently, E-Trade is targeted at high investment value traders and high-value investors.

With E-Trade, you will have access to the most advanced technology in the stock market, with a very simplified selling and buying interface. Any stock you put into your watch list will be visible to you from the mobile application and the website, with real-time price charts provided. Almost 300 ETFs and 4,500 trust funds attract zero commission on E-Trade, but you may not transact internationally.

For the reason that E-Trade seems to favor well-established investors (assets over $250,000) and traders, it may not be a very attractive broker to start you investment journey with. Not even the outstanding training resources and competitive customer service can quite make up for the fact that E-Trade is essentially a traders' broker.

Robinhood

Robinhood is a fairly new stock brokerage service in the market having started in 2017 as a mobile app targeted at the millennial investor. The company has since introduced a website.

Robinhood does not charge any commission on options or stock transactions, which is by far its best feature. This is because no other broker charges zero commission on all trades. Moreover, you can open an account with Robinhood with zero opening balance and no minimum balance required afterwards. The app works in a freemium basis, meaning that you can access basic features for free but you will need to upgrade to a paid account to access some advanced features on a subscription basis. In the case of Robinhood, a $5 monthly fee upgrades you to a Gold account through which you may access better research than the free account and margin borrowing.

Robinhood does not directly execute your buy order. Instead, it sends customer trades to market makers who in turn execute your transaction. Price adjustment means that sometimes the price you get may be higher or lower than the market levels. On the whole, Robinhood seems to be a perfect case of "what you pay is what you get." The skeletal nature of its services- little research of debatable quality, bare minimum news, analysis, and educational material- means that you may not always get the best deal investing with them. But the cost-effectiveness of the whole operation: the Gold account, which is still much cheaper than any other brokerage firm, offers much better support and could actually help you build a respectable investment portfolio even from very small initial capital.

The fundamental difference between Stocks and Bonds

Stocks and bonds are the lifeblood of the economy, but they represent very different ideals. While stocks give the holder a stake in the company for which they have been issued, bonds are simply a tool used by the government to raise short, medium, or long-term debt with a fixed interest rate payable after the maturity of the bond.

Stocks present a higher risk and reward opportunity for investment. The average rate of growth of stocks for NYSE listed companies has been about 7% over the last few decades. Most stocks appreciate faster, at double digit rate, ensuring great reward for investors. However, the risk of a company's fortunes plummeting in the 10-20 years over which an investment may be held makes investing in stocks that much riskier.

Negative growth rates are also quite common in the stock market. For example, by mid-2018, stocks were down an average 5% from the beginning of the year. Stocks perform worse in bear markets, seriously eroding the value of your investment.

Bonds, on the other hand, present lower earnings but greater security compared to stocks. The government is the most common issuer of bonds, using this form of borrowing to finance everything from wars to infrastructural developments. When bonds were first offered about 400 years ago, they were a preserve of national governments. Over the years, however, the accessibility of a large pool of resources has devolved bonds to local governments and large corporations. These new players often issue bonds to raise gargantuan amounts of money that a single bank may not be able to loan them. The bond spreads the risk of the loan to many investors.

Because their use is almost always in developments, returns are almost always guaranteed. As such, bonds are very low-risk and dependable; you are almost guaranteed to never lose money on a bond. However, compared to stocks, bonds are also very low-reward. Yield rates on bonds are always lower than stocks by about 3%, which is a significant amount. The yield rate of bonds is also influenced by the laws of supply and demand in the market and also by the performance of the stock market. Because bonds are seen as being more secure, investors flock to them when the stock market deteriorates, raising yield rates even as stock prices decline. Even though bonds don't grow much, the fact that their value increases (however marginally while stocks prices plummet during a recession) makes them quite attractive.

The US bond market is currently valued at over $41 trillion. Borrowing by the government accounts for about half of this figure, with private entities sharing the rest of it. As for raising money, about 60% of the almost $20 trillion the government owes comes from international lenders (including foreign governments and monetary authorities). The US bond market is also quite active, responsible for about $500 billion worth of transactions every day.

The 2019 bond market has benefitted from innovations that have taken place since the onset of the 21st century. It is very different from the bond market of the 20th century both in its geographical scope and types of bonds traded. In the 1900s, risk premiums for bonds were very low. This was because the government, as the principal bonds borrower, did not need huge loans yet. When the US government was roped into the World War I, there arose a need to borrow heavily to support the war effort. Yield rates were then improved to make bonds more attractive to investors.

After borrowing heavily again for the World War II, the government intentionally kept bond yields low immediately after the war was over to prevent inflation in the event that people cashed in the heavily promoted war bonds. Starting in 1951, the restrictions were lifted. Over the next 30 years, a bull market sent the bond yields climbed rising dramatically to peak at about 15% in 1981.

Starting in the 1970s, the global markets started becoming increasingly unified as globalization raged. The globalization of bond markets was driven by the rise of investments by mutual funds and cross-country retail investors. As stated above, bonds can only be raised for specific expenditures, mostly development efforts. Starting in the 1980s, new classes of assets for which bonds could be issued were established. These included mortgage-backed, high-yield, asset-backed, and inflation-protected securities as well as catastrophic bonds for emergency expenditures.

The first decades of the 21st century further advanced the innovations made to the bond market in the last decades of the 20th century. Asset-backed securities have received particular attention from investors because they present such an attractive money-making opportunity. Any asset with future cash flow potential could now be turned into an asset-backed security. If you go to the bond market today, you will find numerous healthcare receivables, student loans, and mutual fund fees with quite attractive yields.

Trading in these asset classes between institutional investors like banks has also increased significantly. In the 2000s, banks swapped mortgage-backed securities amongst themselves to offset credit defaults and bad interest rates. These swaps have once proven to be quite detrimental, during the crash of 2009. The fact that the bond and equities markets both picked up within a couple of years after one of the world's worst crashes in history proves that investment is always a viable alternative in the long run.

Index Funds

Stock markets often use a select group of stocks to create a general feel for the overall performance of the market. This is commonly known as a stock index. Indexes use market capitalization of listed companies to assign weighs in the index, which means that the biggest companies account for a bigger share of the index than smaller ones. Some of the most prominent indexes include the Dow Jones, the S&P 500, the Wilshire 5,000 Total Market, and the Russell 2000. The value of indexes rises and falls according to the fluctuations in the price of constituent shares in the stock market.

Index funds invest in the whole stock market or a certain portion of it as viewed through the index. As such, an investment in an index fund grows by the average rate of stock price growth of a group of companies. Since share prices move in an upwards trajectory, index funds present a slightly less volatile investment than individual share prices because rises and falls in the share price of individual companies weigh each other up and down. Index funds are considered to be more passive than stocks. Not only are there a few indexes to choose from, but once the fund has identified a basket of stocks to invest in, it remains mostly fixed, with gains being made over the long run.

Before investing in an index fund, you should be clear on the expenses and fees charged by the fund. It is also important to figure out the risks you are likely to face with the collective stocks held. Index funds also tend to be aligned with special interests like clean energy, technology, banking, etc. You should figure out if the investment strategy of the fund aligns with your own goals for investing. Index funds are rather pricey to trade in, with buy and sell transactions attracting up to $50 in commission fees. More predictable growth in index values makes it a more secure investment over ten or more years.

Chapter 3: Financial Management – and how to ensure you get the most for your money

You have decided to set aside a portion of your money for a rainy day. What strategy have you used to decide what percentage to save and how much to invest? Obviously, you can only invest what you don't spend out of your yearly earnings. But if you leave that to chance, you might find yourself investing very little, if anything at all.

Setting a conscious investment goal will allow you to keep yourself in check and hold yourself accountable. There are also financial tools that can guide you through the process. Friends and family can also be invaluable accountability partners in your quest to save up. This book is not meant to teach you how to free up money for investment, but we can give you a few pointers to point you in the right direction.

There are great investment calculator tools online to help you determine how much to invest each month to reach a certain amount by a certain age. To ensure that you don't miss your monthly contribution towards an investment plan, you should prioritize investment over expenditure. Work it so that you take out the amount you need to reach a certain goal by a certain age first, and then pay bills later. Automatic deductions are great for this kind of a plan.

Generally, whatever amount you decide to invest is determined by your total post-tax earnings. A common way to go about deciding the amount of your monthly earnings to invest is the 50/30/20 rule. In this format, 50% of your earnings go towards monthly needs like utilities, rent, groceries, insurance, and other such expenditure. Of course using only 50% of your income in recurrent expenditure may be tough, especially for low income earners. Sort your expenses into need and wants. Groceries, insurance, and utility bills are needs, but cable subscriptions, movies, and other unnecessary expanses and wants. You can do without them.

All these niceties are covered in the 30. After all, you don't work for the future only; it is important that you take care of yourself. 30% of your earnings go into the cable, the spa treatment, drinks out with friends, or any other treats you enjoy that is not strictly necessary for your survival. Of course you may just decide to bundle the 50/30 together into a giant 80, but be careful that the deeper pool of money does not trick you into overspending on either the basics or the secondary needs.

Finally, the 20 goes to your future. A savings plan (in this case investment) is insurance for your future monetary needs. You may maintain an emergency fund, a retirement account, or a special savings plan for a new house, college fund, or any other large expenditure that requires a pile of money. If you have debt, you should use the 20% to pay it off before embarking on an investment path.

The most important thing to keep in mind is that the earlier you start to invest, the better your chances of hitting your target will be. A combination of re-invested dividends, monthly contributions, and capital appreciation boost your initial investment significantly.

Roth IRA & 401K

The Roth IRA and the 401k are retirement accounts. Retirement plans are state sponsored means of ensuring that citizens maintain their living standards even after leaving gainful employment. The time to think about life after employment is during employment, preferably immediately after getting a job offer. That way, your retirement funds accumulate with funds for a longer time.

The 401k retirement plan is an employer-sponsored arrangement where employers and employees each contribute a certain percentage of gross salary. Your contribution to a 401k plan is automated, with employers deducting it from your paycheck each month. The best thing about a 401k plan is the employer contribution. Whatever percentage you decide to invest in your 401k plan your employee will match with a contribution of their own. This is considered free money, but it is probably adjusted in your salary, so view it as your money instead and invest it wisely.

Your employer will also guide you on the best way to invest your 401k funds to ensure maximum benefits. Companies generally select a few options for all their employees to choose from. It is in selecting an investment plan that you should be most careful at. It should be a balance between great returns and risk.

Because the 401k is a long-term plan, you can afford to go with lower interest investments but you definitely cannot afford to lose your retirement plans. You should research widely before deciding how to invest your money. If you get employed at the age of, say 24, and you expect to retire at 65, you are looking at 41 years. And while you are limited to the options your company offers, you can maximize gains by choosing the investment plan with the lowest expense ratio.

Here's the thing though, the government limits the amount of money you can contribute to your 401k up to $18,000 a year. With employer match on contributions, you still get a good annual injection. Like I said before, viewing the employer match on your contribution as "free money" is the wrong strategy. Look at it as money that was most probably factored in the offer you received. It is your money, so the most of it you can get of it the better. Max out on your personal contribution and force your employer to max out on their own contribution; you will thank yourself later.

The Roth IRA –full name Individual Retirement Account- is a private retirement fund formed through an act of congress sponsored by Senator William Roth. The Roth IRA allows you to create your own retirement account with an investment firm. Roth IRAs have limited access even to you. For example, you have to have had the plan for at least five years or be at least 59.5 years old to withdraw from a Roth IRA account. You may also withdraw to buy a house, to settle medical bills, or pay for a child's education.

Unlike the 401k plan, Roth IRA is paid for using your after-tax earnings. Unlike the 401k, you will not be taxed to take money out after the plan matures. Roth IRAs are also better than 401k plans because you are free to invest it in whatever brokerage firm you prefer.

Both the Roth IRA and 401k plans have their advantages and disadvantages. Anyone who tells you that either of these plans is better in different types of taxation environments- higher or lower taxes for higher earnings- is sending you on a fool's errand. It is impossible to predict the direction of taxes 20-30, even 40 years into the future. The only predictable thing about taxation in USA is that Democrat administrations tend to favor higher taxes for the rich and Republicans favor tax cuts. Taxation is highly politicized and since you cannot possibly guess how the political landscape will be shaped in regard to taxation, you should focus on choosing a plan that gives you maximum capital gains. When you are closer to retirement (around 5-10 years) you can gauge the political landscape in regard to taxes and choose the most appropriate course of action. It is too premature to think about withdrawing your funds if the event is 20 years away. Focus on a good investment plan for now.

Chapter 4: Cultivating a Profitable Investing Mindset

You understand Roth IRA and 401k investments. From the brokerage firms reviewed in the previous chapter, you probably have a good idea which one best suits your needs. After looking at your lifestyle and determining how much of your earnings you can set aside for the future, you are eager to start growing your wealth. But are you ready to start investing yet? After all, you are new at this. And you are investing for your future, so you cannot afford to make any mistakes. In this chapter, we focus on transforming you into the outstanding investor you need to be to make it in the stock market

Fundamental Mindset

The stock market may be described using the worlds of Jesse Livermore, also known as the great bear of Wall Street; "financial markets will remain the same yesterday, today, and tomorrow simply because of (human) fear, greed, hope, and ignorance" (Siepmann, 2016).Understanding how these four emotions affect us may be the key to finding success investing in the stock market. More recently, Warren Buffett has simplified the sentiments of Jesse Livermore with the pithy quote; "until you can manage your mind, do not expect to manage money" (Siepmann, 2016).

You must develop within yourself an investor's mindset if you hope to succeed in the field of investment. People are generally emotional beings and the stock market is one of the areas where these emotions directly impact the economy. In the stock market, fear drives people to divest equities in a badly performing stock. Greed steers many investors towards stocks with the greatest potential for future gains, while the hope for future gains is what attracts people to the stock market in the first place. It also keeps them going through the tough spells in the market. Ignorance causes people to hope while they should be fearful and to be fearful when they should be greedy.

Many financial analysts will have you think that you can predict future rises in prices. Many financial analysts are wrong. The only thing you can be confident of while forecasting future stock returns is that you will probably turn out to be wrong. It is impossible to have a 100% record of investing in profit-making stocks. You should expect that a few of your stock picks will perform below expectation. The corollary to that law of financial history is that the markets will most brutally surprise the very people who are most certain that their views about the future are right. The only thing you can do is shore up your stock picks with comprehensive market research.

Coping with Market Volatility

The fact that the stock market fluctuates should not be deterrence to investing. Since your interest in stock prices is long-term, it does not matter that your stock loses value over the short time as long as it picks up and climbs higher than the price at which you bought it. Over the last few years, the stock market has been even more volatile than past decades. Investing has become more of a roller coaster than a train. As an investor, "a roller coaster ride" is the last phrase you would want to use in describing your investment.

Yet volatility is totally and irrevocably unavoidable. Millions of transactions take place on the stock market every day and people who are buying and selling are often reacting to mainstream news and prospects of a company. Traders capitalize on these fluctuations in price to make quick money, but the risks inherent to trading makes it unattractive for passive investors. Traders often have stop-loss measures whereby their stocks are sold automatically when a certain price is reached. Realistically, companies experience periods of massive growth, for example after launching a successful product, followed by an interval of slow economic activity when the market buzz on new products dies down and the company hunkers down to develop new products. This is especially prevalent among electronics products companies, pharmaceuticals, and other such companies.

As an investor, you may deal with market volatility in two ways; continue holding the stocks you own, even when they drop in price, for as long as you are confident the company you bought a stake in remains strong. Another strategy is for the more audacious investor. As long as you remain confident that a company is strong, the times when the share drops in price is a great buying opportunity. You can shore up your investment by buying more shares at lower prices. When the price soars in the future, your investment will grow exponentially as well.

 Keep your ear to the ground on all your volatile stocks. Try as much as possible to access inside information on the future prospects of the company. Mainstream media is not enough to keep you up to date with the goings-on behind the scene that indicate the strength of a company. Subscribe to trade journals and company newsletters. Research deep and wide on the industry your company operates in. Understand their business model and business practices. Armed with all this information, you can make informed decisions on the future of the company regardless of the mainstream media and the market reaction that follows.

Another very effective strategy to cope with market volatility is to diversify. Rather than investing in one company, create a stock portfolio of a group of companies you understand and believe in. That way, you will monitor the portfolio as a whole as your primary concern and the individual stocks as a secondary matter. You will effectively have created your own personal index fund of rigorously researched companies and as discussed in the previous chapter, index funds are generally more stable over the long run. A portfolio will also save you those heart lurches every time one stock drops in price because another stock will probably gain simultaneously and cancel out the decline.

For example, if you only hold shares in Exxon Mobil, your investment will go down when oil prices drop because Exxon shares will drop along with them. However, if you leverage this stock with Ford Motors, a car company whose shares react in the opposite direction of low oil prices, the portfolio will remain stable. Since these two companies are strong overall, their shares will continue to grow over the long term so your portfolio will obviously appreciate.

Seems like quite a lot of work, doesn't it? Well, the alternative is to keep your money in the bank at below inflation interest, losing purchasing power in the long run. It may seem daunting at first, but as you grow into stock investing, you will actually enjoy the excitement. What's more, your investment will grow at rates a bank simply could not provide you.

Market bubbles

Market bubbles form when the price of a commodity rises beyond its market value over a short time. Bubbles are unique in that they defy the basic laws of demand and supply. It is not because a commodity is highly sought after that its price rises. It is because investors speculate on the future prices beyond common sense levels. Because numerous investors are putting their money on a commodity at once, the price rises sharply. The fate of a bubble is always bursting, with investors losing money because buyers are unwilling to pay for the inflated value attributed to a commodity.

To understand just how insane bubbles can be, consider the fact that the first reported bubble occurred back in the 1600s in the Netherlands on the price of tulips. Their price was so high that at the peak of tulip-mania, one tulip contract could be traded for a house. When the bubbles popped, "tulip investors" lost an insane amount of money. While bubbles do not form over such mundane commodities today- they form instead on real estate, a certain stock, or other trendsetting commodities- they are still extremely risky. And they end in the same way; a burst bubble and massive losses for the tulip investors.

Bubbles usually follow the same stages from inception to bursting. The first step is displacement, in which investors become captivated by a new concept, product, or technology. Gradually, the commodity takes off, driven by rising interest and demand by investors. In this first stage, the smart investors invest heavily, further rending credence to the investment fervor. Soon, institutional investors join the fray. Increasing interest drives up interest and thus the gains made by initial investors. The rate of growth in value of the commodity remains normal by market standards and there is little cause for alarm.

Exponential growth in commodity prices generate massive buzz. At this stage, you may start to see the stories of 'average investors' who moved from rags to riches by investing in the product in the media. A boom follows, with prices rising faster and faster every day. Spurred by the fear of missing out, investors pump money into the commodity with little consideration for its real value or potential as an investment. The public joins the fray and the product slowly becomes over-invested.

A euphoric atmosphere soon develops; sending prices even higher. Valuation metrics may be developed to rationalize the unreasonable prices and unrelenting rise in prices. At this point, people are no longer investing in a financial product. It is a once-in-a-lifetime opportunity to make dizzying amounts of money. The only people who really make money are the smart investors who put money into the product in the initial stages. Most of them sell at this point, cashing in on the gains made so far on their investments and motivating new entrants to invest too.

This stage of the bubble is called the profit-taking stage. Smart money investors, sensing an impending burst, divest off their holdings and make a killing. Profit-taking is an inevitable stage of a bubble and because it precedes the burst, it is important for the investors who have kept their wits around them through the unreasonable price hikes to sell, because the next stages will whittle their investments to below their market value. The challenge lays in determining when the burst may occur. After witnessing their investments rise ten, sometimes hundreds of times, even the smart investors may get trapped in the once-in-a-lifetime moneymaking opportunity, wanting to capitalize as much as possible on any gains.

Finally, the market realizes that the price of the inflated commodity does not match up with their unreasonable expectations. Prices level off because new investors stop joining the fray as fast as they were doing before. With no new buyers, prices plummet. The effect of every investor trying to liquidate their holdings at the current rates is such a steep drop in prices that the commodity sells at less than its real value before the bubble. Late entrants suffer particularly terrible losses, being the fodder from which initial investors make their fat gains.

As an investor, you can avoid the risk of decimating your investing through a bubble by following one very simple principle; *do not become a tulip investor.* Do not follow the market buzz, especially if you cannot find underlying economic reasons for an asset class, a stock, or commodity to be so highly priced. Lower assured gains are better than sky-high fictional profits.

Timing the market

Market timing is the investment tactic whereby investors purport to figure out the best time to invest and divest to make higher gains on investment. Investors then use their predictions to determine the best times to sell or buy. However, the tactic may backfire with serious repercussions because changes in the market occur randomly and unpredictably. A stock may gain when you expected it to lose in value and vice versa. The greatest risk market timers face is losing out on great market cycles because your forecasts predicted tough times and the market picked up instead. Good stocks appreciate over time, picking up even after experiencing a spell of price decline.

And while market timing is not the solution to market volatility, neither is complacence. It is very irresponsible to not track the progress of your stock. Time is your friend, so as long as you are sufficiently informed and your research shows that a company in which you hold stock remains strong, there is no reason to keep moving your stocks around. If in doubt, consult a financial advisor. They always know what is what when it comes to the stock market.

To remove the emotion from your investment process and help you build your wealth, you should consider using dollar-cost averaging while building your stock portfolio. In dollar-cost averaging, you buy shares worth a fixed amount of money over a long time. With dollar-cost averaging, you will get to enjoy the benefits of dips and rises in stock prices without the adversities of price fluctuations. When the price of a stock is low, you buy more shares with the same amount of money. At higher prices, you can afford fewer shares but your portfolio grows because you have already bought a substantial amount at a lower price.

Dollar-cost averaging is used by the gurus of stock investing because they represent such a genius idea in hedging your bets as an investor. As an example, let's assume that you have dedicated $100 every month to buying shares in company Q. In the first month, the shares trade at $20 and you buy 5 shares. The second month the price drops to $10, affording you 10 shares. In total, you have managed to buy 15 shares at $200. If you had bought shares worth the cumulative $200 at $20, you would only have gotten 10 shares, but by staggering your purchase points, you manage to buy 15 shares at the bargain price of $13.3.

Dollar-cost averaging allows the investor to buy more shares when the price is lower. And while it does not always assure you the best bargains in this endeavor, it presents you with the opportunity to buy at the average price; not too high and not too low. Working with your stock broker, you can build your portfolio by automatically buying stocks when they go below the value of your initial buying price. With a selection of stocks to consider, you can always be assured of a bargain in buying more shares of a company in your portfolio. Again, you will have to ensure than any of the stocks that you target are good enough to reduce anxiety in buying when the prices go down.

In essence, dollar-cost averaging removes an investor's anxiety over what price presents the best buying opportunity. There will always be fears that the price is not low enough to give you the gains you may desire. A staggered price through DCA enables you to take the emotions out of investing. You would have fewer regrets if you bought $1,000 worth of shares at two batches of $78 and $63than if you bought at $78 and then the price dropped to $63. Even if you are buying for the long run and the price rises to $100 over time, you will always regret losing the $15 bargain per share. Even though you will buy less shares overall with $500 than with $1,000, the fact that you capitalized on lower prices to shore up your investment will be a little bit more satisfying. Those wins (buying shares at lower prices) once every while will be very motivating in the long run and will make you ever more eager to invest on a regular basis.

I cannot stress enough how important it is to perform your due diligence research on a company before investing in it. It is the only way you can remain confident enough to keep buying more shares at lower prices for better gains when the market improves. So what exactly informs the recommended bullish attitude towards price drops? What do you need to know to buy when everyone else is selling without worrying about losing your investment? The next chapter covers these questions and more in full depth.

Chapter 5: Fundamental vs. Technical analysis of stocks –
which is more effective for the novice investor?

In the first chapter of this book, you were introduced to value investing, the investing strategy that actively seeks out stocks that the rest of the stock market places little value in. With value investing, panic selling in the market presents a great opportunity to buy. In the words of Warren Buffett, value investing entails "being greedy when others are being fearful (and) fearful when everyone else is being greedy (Wallstreet Mojo, 2019)." As you may have gathered from previous sub-topics, value investing is grounded in the objective analysis of a company's future prospects in a process known as due diligence. Due diligence helps you acquaint yourself with the business because the things you don't know about a company is what most often losses you money.

Due Diligence

In conducting a due diligence investigation for a company in whose stock you are interested in investing, start by looking at the market capitalization. Companies with a large market capitalization are often better to invest in because their stock price holds steady over time. Another thing to find out in the first step of your due diligence is where the company is traded. This allows you to find out if can buy shares from the company through your brokerage firm.

The second step in due diligence studies is the numbers. You will need to find out how the company's revenue, profit, and margin hold up. The balance sheet is a great place to start because it presents all these financial details in one document. Listed companies are required to release their financial reports the public, so it should not be too much of a hustle locating it. In the balance sheet, the key areas to consider include short term liabilities, cash flows, and long term debt. A great idea is to start with the last two years and go as far back as you possibly can, especially if you are considering the company for long-term investment.

Future prospects of a company are shaped in more ways than one by the rest of the market. If the industry is undergoing massive growth, the company is likely to perform well. On the other hand, stiff competition tends to create more volatility. Understand the business environment in which the company operates. Get a feel for the market and future prospects. Even though you cannot pinpoint future changes, you can definitely predict future growth in an industry. Is your prospective company positioned to benefit from market changes? You should feel confident enough about its market placement.

The management of a company plays a huge part in its financial performance. Younger companies are often run by founding members while older ones focus on experienced bosses. The experience of senior managers is a big determinant on the present and future financial health of a company. You should also look into their share ownership of senior managers in the company. Your interests as a shareholder will be better served by a person who stands to lose or gain if the shares drop or rise. For younger companies with founders in management positions, low percentage share ownership by managers is especially alarming and might even be a red flag. On share ownership, look for institutional investors because they indicate widespread optimism on the company's future prospects. Institutional investors also generate greater publicity for a stock in the market; a plus because greater publicity often means more people investing, so the price rises.

It goes without saying, but the history of the company's stock price is a very important consideration. It gives you a rough idea of changes you might expect and most importantly, it discloses just how volatile the company's shares are. Also consider the likelihood of the company being diluted and the stock options offered. A company that gives employees stock options tends to perform well because the labor force is fully vested. While checking out the stock options, look out for investigations by the Securities and Exchange Commission (SEC). Companies accused on stock malpractices like options backdating tend to be riskier and more volatile.

Finally, while you cannot predict future stock prices, you can watch out for the signs that indicate possible increase in revenue. Do some extra digging and find out if there are possible joint ventures, new products, or partnerships in the offing. If there are any of these three items in the near future of the company, then you can be a little more confident in the financial future of the company and thus its shares.

Some of the due diligence investigations you will need to do involve more than just perusing through a balance sheet. You will need to go deep and look into those micro and macroeconomic factors that most affect financial performance in a company. You will need to do fundamental and technical analysis. Only through fundamental and technical analysis can you gain the unshakeable confidence you need to engage in value investing.

Fundamental vs. Technical Analysis

Fundamental analysis is a measure of a stock's real qualitative and quantitative value calculated from its financial records. It is only through fundamental analysis that you can find out if a share is valued lower or higher from its intrinsic value. Fundamental analysis starts big and goes minute so that all details can be unearthed and studied.

The objective of fundamental analysis is to come up with a fair stock price for a company based on its intrinsic value and number of shares issued. The fair stock price is then used to determine if a stock is overvalued or undervalued in the stock market. The decision to buy or sell is then made based on this assessment. You buy if the fair price is lower than the market price, because the price will most assuredly climb. If the fair price is higher than the market price, then divestment is a valid idea because sooner or later the stock will fall back to its fair price.

Fundamental analysis can also be used to make buy and sell decisions on other types of securities like bonds. The state of the economy, interest rates, and the credit rating of the issuer are the things to look out for when conducting fundamental analysis on a bond. The metrics used in fundamental analysis are external in nature compared to technical analysis; the economy, company management, the strengths, weaknesses, opportunities, and threats (SWOT) of a company all paint a picture of the company in the context of the industry.

Technical analysis, on the other hand, is a detailed study of the company internals like price, volumes, patterns, support and resistance stock price levels, and recognition. The aim of technical analysis is to predict future prices by looking at trends and patterns of stock prices in the past.

Technical analysis observes patterns in price changes to disclose the strengths and weaknesses of a stock and make it easier for traders to recognize the best points at which to sell or buy more shares. Technical analysis is inherently short-term price prediction strategy that disregards the company's essentials to focus solely on its stock price. In technical analysis, efficient market hypothesis (EMH) teaches you to assume that the fair price of a stock is equal to its market value, so you focus on changes in price in your evaluations. Another assumption of technical analysis proposed by Charles Dow is that changes in the price of a stock happen in a certain pattern that remains steady over time.

Technical analysis places a lot of emphasis on the stock market valuation of the company and may be subject to mass thought prejudices. When the market takes unfounded interest in a company's stock and buys more with no underlying reason, technical analysis will pick that up and factor it into the buy/sell recommendation. Fundamental analysis, on the other hand, seeks to be grounded in fact, so it analyzes the nuts and bolts of a company.

Clearly then, technical analysis is a trading tool while fundamental analysis is for the everyday investor interested in learning about more than just the stock price changes of their held companies. With fundamental analysis, you are assured of gaining a wholesome understanding of the company that is essential for those value investments, especially in those low stock price periods when technical analysis may be advising selling.

Remember this - it is better to buy a great company at a fair price than it is to buy a fair company at a great price. Great companies are good for the long run, but fair companies might disappoint you.

Since this is a book about investment, we will now look further into fundamentals analysis and the financial ratios that indicate value investment opportunities.

Earnings per share (EPS)

The Earnings per Share ratio is a financial measure that indicates the overall profitability of a business. To get the EPS, you divide the company's net after tax income with all issued shares. As such, the EPS represents the profit allocation for every share.

Shares with higher EPS values are considered more lucrative. A variation of the EPS ratio is the weighted earnings per share ratio which subtracts total dividends from the total earnings. The weighted EPS gives a more accurate picture of a company's profitability and should be used in the place of the EPS for companies that issues dividends to shareholders. This is because weighted EPS indicates possible future increases in dividends issued by a company.

P/E ratios

The price-to-earnings ratio compares a company's market value to its earnings. The P/E indicates the value the stock market places on a company's past, present, and future earnings prospects. The higher the P/E, the more likely it is that the company's stock is overvalued. Lower P/E ratios indicate possibly undervalued companies, which might be a great opportunity for value investing. However, you should not hurry to buy based on the P/E ratio alone. The decision to buy should be informed by the careful consideration of a company's overall financial strength.

Looking into the performance of a few other companies in the industry may also give you a reference point to determine just how undervalued or overvalued the stock is. If the P/E is high relative to other companies in the industry, it may be caused by greater confidence in its future by the stock market and thus be overvalued. If it is lower, chances are it is undervalued, an opportunity for value investing.

Another way to calculate the P/E ratio is by comparing the stock price with the EPS. This alternative to calculating EPS is a little more complex, but it gives a more comprehensive idea of a company's value. As an investor, you want to invest in a company that has a good return on investment. The P/E ratio is one of the many financial ratios through which you can figure out if your stock is fairly priced.

Return on Equity (RoE)

Return on equity (ROE) is a variation of the return on equity ratio that measures the effectiveness of a company's management to generate profits using existing assets. It measures the success of a company in rewarding shareholders with profits. The RoE is calculated by dividing earnings after tax with total equity and multiplying by 100% to find the percentage RoE. Companies with higher RoE are traded more in the market because investors are assured of earnings. Financial analysts recommend investing in stocks with more than 12% rate of return on equity.

Price to Book Ratio

The price-to-book ratio is the ultimate indicator of what the market thinks of a company's prospects versus the reality. To find price-to-book ratio, you will need to divide the book value per share of company by its market price.

Book value indicates the balance sheet net worth of a company. To calculate book value, the company is viewed as an asset and the value of accumulated intangible assets like goodwill and patents and liabilities is taken out. The book value per share is calculated by dividing the book value with the total number of outstanding shares. Market price is simply the going rate for one share of the company's stock in the market. Dividing these two values gives the P/B ratio.

Just as with the P/E ratio, a lower ratio relative to the rest of the industry indicates a possibly undervalued stock. The P/B ratio is analyzed along with return on equity, an indicator of expected returns on every dollar invested in a company's stock. If the difference between the P/B ration and the ROE is too huge, then the stock may not be all that attractive for investing.

Debt to Equity Ratio

The debt to equity ratio is also known as the risk ratio. The main objective of the debt to equity ratio is to disclose whether a company's capital structure is more debt or equity based. It assesses the weight of a company's liabilities on shareholder equity. A company with debts totaling $50 million and equity of $240 million would have a debt to equity ratio of 0.42. Such a company can comfortably cover its liabilities using its assets and is more likely to be a stable investment.

Higher debt to equity ratios indicate highly leveraged companies- a red flag for declining companies. However, stable companies with good cash flows are better served by high debt to equity ratios because they are able to use debt to increase the return on equity. Equity is more expensive capital than debt, so higher D/E ratios indicate that a company is raising capital at a cheaper overall cost. As long as the debt ratio is maintained at a manageable level, higher D/E ratios indicate stocks with better RoE and thus a great opportunity for investment.

You can get all these fundamental analysis information and a whole bunch of technical data from the internet. Financial statistics are updated in real time in numerous websites for your easy access. On bloomberg.com, you will find statistics on energy and agricultural companies from the U.S., Europe, and Asia. *Bloomberg* also features statistics on commodities, bonds, futures, and currencies. You can also view economic calendars on impending events that affect the stock market and be informed in advance.

Yahoo! Finance is another great source of real time stock prices and international news. Just like *Bloomberg, Yahoo! Finance* shows news from Asia, Europe, and the US. Top financial stories and analyst opinions are also featured on the homepage for easy perusal. An added advantage of viewing financial data on *Yahoo! Finance* is their stock comparison feature that allows you to compare historical prices of a stock against the industry or other stocks.

The Wall Street Journal is one of the most prominent financial magazines that reports on the stock market. Not only does *The Wall Street Journal* allow you to view prices going back several decades, it also gives you the choice to download spreadsheets for offline analysis at your leisure.

Another important website is the *Financial Times*. You may need to create an account to access some information like historic prices from the site, but you may not download data from *Financial Times* like with *The Wall Street Journal*.

Other sites worth checking out include *Simple Wall Street*, *Microsoft Money*, *Morningstar*, *Google Finance*, and *Kitco* among others.

Chapter 6: An Introduction to Dividends – The Lifeblood of Any Investor

If the objective of investing is to maximize capital gains on initial and additional investments. Then the best way to maximize your investment is to buy stocks that reward shareholders with dividends. Dividend-paying companies are the only worthwhile ones to invest in because your money actively generates earnings for you without you having to sell off your initial investment.

What are dividends?

Dividends are defined as the share of profits that shareholders receive from a company for owning equity in the company. It is essentially the money that a company pays you for providing them with capital and you are entitled to earn it. The dividend given on every share is known as the dividend yield and is paid annually, mostly around the time the company releases its financial report. A company decides whether to reward shareholders with all its accumulated profits and earnings for the year or to reinvest a portion of it into the business. Because the board of directors determines the portion of profits and retained earnings to distribute to shareholders, dividend yields vary from year-to-year depending on the financial needs of the company. Higher profits do not necessarily mean higher rewards, because the board of directors may opt to reinvest more of it into the business.

There are several types of dividends payable to shareholders. The first and most common type is actual cash being paid directly from the company and injected into the shareholders' account. You as the investor will then decide what to do with this cash: reinvest into the same company, invest in another stock, or put the money into other types of use. Dividends are capital gains to be used in whatever way you as the investor prefer.

Another way a company may pay dividends is by issuing shareholders with new shares based on the number of shares owned in the company. The direct opposite of this strategy is called the share buyback in which the company buys shares from shareholders from annual profits. A share buyback gives money back to shareholders in exchange for their shareholdings. The overall effect of this kind of transaction is that the remaining stockholdings are consolidated in both value and EPS.

Some companies pay dividends in the form of assets like physical assets, real estate, or investment securities of other kinds. Because the company will be buying these assets in bulk to distribute to their shareholders, you may get them at prices below market level and watch as your dividend bears even more returns for you over the long term.

A company may opt to pay dividends when it accumulates excess cash and the scheduled dividend pay-out date is still a long way away. This type of dividend is called a special dividend and it may be paid quarterly, bi-annually, or once every few years.

Not every dividend stock is a good buy, obviously. As an investor, you need to have a checklist of all the qualities you need in a dividend to make you buy. By combining common sense ideas and financial wisdom, we have come up with 8 rules for you to follow in picking a dividend stock to buy.

The first rule is that you should only buy shares in strong companies with a proven track record of profit-making, expansion, and consistency. It is much better to buy a strong stock at a fair price than it is to buy a fair stock at a great price. Quality businesses have quality shares and quality shares make for quality investments, especially over the long term. Dig into the company's financial records and unearth the dividend payouts going back two decades ago or more if possible. If you look at the S&P 500, you will discover that stocks that have been paying rising dividends over the last 25 years perform better than other companies by 2.88%.

The second rule is called the bargain rule. It states that you should only invest in companies with higher dividend returns per share. This rule is the value investing principle of buying dividend stocks. By picking out a stock at its lowest price and dividend-yield, you will see growth in both the stock and the dividend yield in future. Downturns are unavoidable in business, especially in sectors like energy, healthcare, the financial markets, and other critical sectors of the economy. Industries that are affected by government policies are especially fraught with instability, but sluggish growth does not always mean that a company is doomed to fail. Overpriced securities will hardly ever give you good returns. They are also very risky, because upwards growth just means more overpricing and a probable collapse in price sooner or later. Stocks trading at lower historical averages but still maintaining high dividend yields are the best you could buy. Stocks with a strong foundation but currently underperforming in both dividend yield and stock price, comes in a close second.

Just because you are encouraged to chase better and increasing dividend yields does not mean you should go for the company that breaks its bank vaults to reward your investment in them. This is the third rule. You should look out for the margin of safety, which is the cash reserve a company opts to not distribute to shareholders as dividends but instead to use in expanding the business. Under this rule, you recognize that businesses experience slumps that may bring the dividend down. The duration and seriousness of the slump varies from industry to industry, but it is a reality of the economy and should not be a discouragement from purchasing stock. A share repurchasing policy is a great indication of a company that is bullish about its future. It may also indicate undervalued shares.

The fourth rule is that growth is very important in the stock market. From the first, this book has taught you to invest for the long run. Dividends contribute to the long term investment, but the stock growth percentage remains to be an important consideration. A decade or two of consistent stock price growth is a great indication of the potential your investment has to grow in the future. Dividend per share growth is also a very important metric. Companies with rising dividend payouts have done 2.4% better than those with stagnant dividend in the last 40 years.

The fifth rule is that you should only invest in businesses that can hold steady even through recessions and market panics. You are not starting to invest as your full-time career; you still have your day job. Investing is a savings plan for the future, assuring you of a comfortable lifestyle when you will no longer be productive. It gives you the security of knowing that your future is well taken care of. During recessions, many stocks plummet because people sell and invest in other more stable and confidence-inspiring businesses. Go for these businesses because only then can you rest easy even in the worst market upheavals.

The sixth rule deals with selling dividend shares. Even though you should only buy stocks that pay good dividends, the dividend payments will still be much lower than your total investment in that company. You should keep one eye on the dividend and another on your principal. The financial ratios discussed in the previous chapter are not just for stock-buying purposes. A stock should remain attractive enough that you would still want to buy it at its current price. And if you bought an undervalued stock, look out for when it becomes overvalued. Financial experts recommend selling when the P/E ratio climbs higher than 40 because rarely will a company climb higher than that. Stocks with smaller P/E ratios perform better than those with high P/E's by almost 10%. That is a lot. So the rule is; if an undervalued stock is a great buying opportunity, then an overvalued stock should also become a sell signal at a certain level. This level is P/E ratios above 40.

The seventh rule is keeping your eyes open for trouble. The worst thing you can do in the stock market is to keep your eyes closed to the facts. Just because a company was a good investment opportunity last year does not make it great now. Reduction in dividend payments is a sign of trouble. Complete elimination of dividends is a warning signal that your company can no longer compete. The S&P 500 index shows 0% returns from companies that had eliminated or cut down on dividend yields in the last 4 decades.

The eighth and last rule of dividend investment is called the diversification principle. Unless you can be confident of being 100% right all the time, then you should hedge your bets by investing in a few different companies. Alternatively, you can go all out and invest in completely different industries. Diversification ensures that you have a lot of options for those times when an underperforming or outstretched stock reaches its zenith of returns and you have to sell to protect your current earnings. With a portfolio, you can move your money around your stocks, investing more in companies with more promising returns to boost your overall investment value. An ideal portfolio size is around 15 stocks.

Why do companies pay dividends?

As stated above, the dividend is what a company pays you for investing in them. You are entitled to that money and you should expect to be paid handsomely for the money you put into a company. In fact, you should not even consider buying a stock if the company does not pay dividends. If a stock does not pay dividends, then it is essentially a speculation in the future price. Stock prices are subject to fluctuations. Therefore, if money will only be made by selling at a higher price in the future, investors will turn into price-watchers likely to divest their stake at the earliest sign of falling prices. The stock will thus become more volatile.

Listed companies have two options; reinvest all profits into the business or use a portion of the earnings to reward shareholders for providing them with capital. So why do they choose to give away money that could otherwise be used to expand the business even further? After all, it is not compulsory to pay dividends. One reason given above is to reduce volatility in the stock price.

Another reason has something to do with the most important piece of advice you should take out of this book; *do not invest in a company that does not pay dividends.* The dividend is what makes a stock attractive as an investment opportunity. It represents extra income that adds to the principle gains on your initial investment and when re-invested, substantially boosts your money. Dividends make the stock more attractive to investors. And because the stock market is just like any other industry with the investor as the customer, paying dividends is one way for companies to attract investors.

But just because a stock pays dividends does not mean that you should blindly put your money into it. Even for the dividend itself, there are several important things to consider. First, what is the dividend per share? Most companies give between 2-5% of the share value in dividends. Anything above 3% is acceptable. Also, how regular are the dividends? Has the company missed out on a payment recently? Missing out on a dividend might be an indication of financial difficulties. Companies often slash the dividend per share when earnings decline, so you should look out for that as well. An increase in the dividend payout indicates confidence in the company's future prospects.

Companies who have historically paid dividends

Very few companies pay dividends at attractive levels. Out of a cumulative 1,500 stocks in the S&P 500, S&P 400 Mid-Cap, and S&P Small-Cap 600 indices, only 199 had a yield above 3.5% as of June 30, 2018. Even fewer companies consistently increase dividend payouts year-on-year. Out of the 199 stocks, only 29 had increased their dividend payout by more than 10% in the past year. Assessing the stocks based on their consistency in making dividend payments in the past 10 years, only 10 companies fulfilled this requirement.

Some of the biggest companies that have historically paid dividends include General Electric, Proctor & Gamble, McDonalds, Disney, and ExxonMobil. On the shorter end of the historic dividend-paying spectrum we have companies like AstraZeneca PLC.

General Electric

General Electric is one of the most popular traded companies in the U.S. The company's shares change hands faster than any other listed company per session, with up to 150 million shares being traded every day. The reason for this is that at around $10, the GE share price is much lower than other blue chip companies. Fluctuations of as low as $0.1 in stock prices represent a bigger percentage loss or gain than a similar fluctuation for a more costly stock.

GE has entrenched itself in American corporate culture in its 127 years of existence as a strong business, first in the lighting and electric products market, and later in a long list of diversified holdings in energy, finance, aviation, healthcare, defense contracting, gas, electric motors, and oil. Having a diversified business model has made GE strong enough to withstand massive disruptions and upheavals (internal and external) that would have floored a less resilient company.

In the last couple of years, GE has been the subject of unrelenting negative publicity as the company has continually missed earnings targets and posed losses quarter after quarter. Just last year, the company was removed from the S&P 20 index after more than 100 years. In the past 10 years, the company has made three dividend cuts. The company gave a measly one penny in its last dividend payout or less than 1% of share price. Whether the company will survive the upheaval experienced in the past one decade or so remains to be seen.

Even though GE is currently performing very poorly, its vast holdings in different industries means that the company is, by and large, insured from possible total failure. One serious restructuring and leadership change is all it would take to turn the company around and make it profitable. GE violates some of the rules for buying dividend stocks discussed earlier in this chapter, but it definitely qualifies for the bargain rule. By all indications, GE is headed for huge growth in both price and dividend yield.

And appearing in this listing of companies that have historically paid dividends, General Electric illustrates that every company encounters downturns. But if you have invested for the long term, then these downturns should not cause you to panic and sell at a lower price. Eventually, the strong ones will rise back again and go back to their money-making ways.

McDonald's

McDonald's is one of the most stable stocks in the market right now. In its last dividend payout, McDonald's gave a yield of 2.4% of the share price, a rate well above average. Insofar as consistency is considered, McDonald's has not just paid, but increased its dividend payout each year for the past 40 years. The stock also performs extremely well in the market, driven by strong sales in established outlet and new restaurants opening up all over the world. The cash flows at McDonald's have never been an issue. The company has enough cash to comfortably increase dividends every year and boost other areas of the business for even better future earnings.

Disney

The Walt Disney Company has been one of the most outstanding entertainment companies in the world ever since its inception in 1923. From Mickey Mouse, to Snow White, to the Disney World amusement parks, Disney has grown to become an integral part of US culture.

While Disney has not achieved the status of Dividend Aristocrat (stocks that have been paying dividends for 25 straight years) yet, its record of 8successive years is very promising. At just

1.5% dividend yield, Disney is modest by industry standards. However, the dividend represents 25% of its earnings, leaving the company with a massive cash endowment to grow its core business for even greater earnings. The capital has enabled Disney to stun the industry with some bold power moves such as the recent acquisition of 21ˢᵗ Century Fox. The acquisition will boost Disney's movie distribution infrastructure and expand the reach of its movies, further increasing earnings and thus the dividend yield.

Procter & Gamble

Procter & Gamble (PG) owns some of the best packaged consumer products brands around the world. Some of its most prominent brands include Gillette, Pampers, Tide, Charmin, Febreze, and Vicks. The PG stock has been one of the best performing dividend shares of the last 6 decades, with a 62-year dividend growth streak. The company currently awards 2.9% of the stock with a P/E ratio of 21.3 in 2019. PG is not undervalued, but it has very good fundamentals. The balance sheet is well-adjusted with sustainable debt and healthy cash flows, which indicates strength in its core business.

On the share price, PG made a return on equity of about 16.3% in the full year ending in December 2018. It is currently on course to match this RoE and probably surpass it. However, the biggest confidence booster about the PG stock is that it is in the stock portfolio of legendary investor Warren Buffett. With a net worth of about $90 billion made entirely from the stock market, you can be confident that Buffett knows a thing or two about healthy investments.

Exxon Mobil

Exxon Mobil is a descendant of Standard Oil, one of America's (and the world's) biggest oil companies. At 137 years, Exxon has one of the longest records of consistently paying dividends in the S&P 500. And with a yield of 3.8% of stock price, Exxon's stock yield is higher than most other stocks in the stock market. Furthermore, the Exxon dividend yield has been increasing for the past 35 years, through the financial crisis and other industry ups and downs. Exxon is considered a dividend aristocrat, a tag reserved for the most outstanding dividend stocks.

AstraZeneca PLC

AstraZeneca is a British-Swedish pharmaceuticals and biotechnology business that is listed in the New York, London, and Stockholm stock exchanges. The most attractive thing about AstraZeneca as a dividend stock is its outstanding rate of yield return. Its average dividend yield in the last 10 years has been a mind-blowing 4.66%, which puts it in the top 25% of companies that pay the best dividends. The company has also been consistent its dividend payout in the past 10 years, which is a confidence-inspiring achievement.

However, the percentage of earnings given as dividends may be a little unsustainable at 91%. Ultimately, AstraZeneca might be forced to cut dividends to cushion the business from fluctuations in earnings or for R&D. On the other hand, AstraZeneca's share price has been rising steadily over the years as investors reacted positively to the rising dividend yields. The above average dividend yields and steady growth in stock price makes Astra very attractive for investing in.

How to get your dividends to pay you twice

Companies reward their shareholders with dividends as an incentive to attract more investment. As stated before, dividends may be paid in the form of cash, shares, or other assets. When dividends are given in the form of shares, it amounts to a reinvestment in the company, because the shareholder is taking their share of earnings and using the money to buy more shares in the same company. Dividend reinvestment programs (DRIPs) are initiated by a company to allow shareholders to invest their dividends back into the company for additional share holdings of the investor and retained earnings for the company.

Dividend payouts are basically cash flows out of the company. If a business intends to keep their earnings for internal operations but still share them with their shareholders, a DRIP is an easy way to accomplish that. Some dividend reinvestment programs follow the tenets of dollar cost averaging by giving the shareholder the chance to buy shares at regular intervals. The only difference with DRIP is that the amount of money put into the buying of stocks is not determined by the investor. The company controls that by setting the dividend yield.

The biggest advantage of DRIP is that the investor does not have to go through stock brokers. As such, there is no commission charged for shares bought. Moreover, companies usually discount the shares awarded through dividend reinvestment programs to give the investor a better deal. Under DRIP, an investor will buy more shares per dollar than when they do it through the open market. And because the dividend entitled to investors will probably not be enough to buy a particular number of shares, a new system of stocks transacting called fractional shareholding was introduced. With fractional shareholding, an investor is allowed to own half shares depending on the amount of money they have. Fractional shares are valuable and count towards an investor's overall holdings and dividend entitlement in a company, but they may not be traded in the open market. The fact that DRIP shares cannot be traded in the open market but are still entitled to future dividends for the shareholder allows listed companies to reduce the volatility of their shares because shareholders are more likely to hold on to these shares.

However, some companies, like British American Tobacco, require their shareholders to retain, at zero interest rate, any extra dollars that are not enough to buy a full share within their accounts until the next DRIP payout. The amount is then added on and used to buy all full shares. The money retired to your DRIP account in this way, anything from $35-$40 on a stock like BAT's, is too much for you to keep it, interest-free, for up to one year until the next dividend payout to get full shares. Even $10 is a lot of money to keep lying around at zero-interest rates, especially in an investment account. Be sure to read all the terms of a company's dividend reinvestment program to avoid falling into a trap like this. And since you will be taxed on the total value of the dividends earned anyway, you might as well make sure that they are put into some moneymaking use as soon as you earn them. Oh yes, the government still views your reinvested dividends as taxable income on which you should expect to pay a capital gain tax.

Another thing to be wary of is the terms of eligibility for reinvestment programs. In some cases, not all investors may be allowed to take advantage of DRIPS. New investors, for example, might be ineligible. Shareholders below a certain level may also be locked out of DRIP, and sometimes companies restrict the types of investors who can access dividend investment programs. The restrictions are especially common among companies that intend to buy some shares back at a future date. But if you qualify, you should definitely sign up for DRIP. Signing up for automatic dividend reinvestment protects you as the investor from being diluted. Being protected from dilution during a stock buyback is very profitable, because your outstanding shares become so much more valuable.

However, you should be careful not to get trapped in a buy and forget situation with one stock and forget to diversify. This would result in overinvestment and reliance in one company, a risky move should the company run into financial difficulties and cause your stock to lose value. It is a whole different ballgame when you receive your dividends in cash form and decide what to do with it; reinvest in the same stock through a stockbroker or buy a different one.

On the whole, a dividend reinvestment program is a great opportunity for you as an investor to consolidate your holdings in a company by buying shares without a middleman- the broker. Not only do you get a nominal fee for the transaction, you also enjoy great discounts on every stock bought. Just be sure that your DRIP does not have a clause that requires you to hold money that is not enough to buy a full share in your DRIP account interest free. Fractional shareholding is a much more attractive idea, even if you don't get to trade those shares in the open market and are limited to redeeming their value through the company.

Chapter 7: Diversification and Risk Management

Why diversification is necessary

No investment is 100% assured to give returns. There is always a chance that the company whose shares you bought will face tough financial times and see dropping share prices. In the worst case scenario, a stock loses so much of its value that your investment is whittled down to just a fraction of the principle. If you are using your investment portfolio as a means of saving for the future, you need to protect it from possible losses. You need to diversify.

Diversification is the simple act of investing in a few assets to regulate the risk exposure of any one asset. With diversification, you stop investing in one company and accumulate an investment portfolio with assets with potential for appreciation over time. These include the stocks discussed so far in previous chapters as well as REITs, International Indexes, emerging markets, and ETFs. These investments will be discussed latter in this chapter.

Any time the price of a stock or other asset drops or rises, the current value (the amount of money you would receive if you were to liquidate today) of your investment goes up and down along with it. These fluctuations can be very nerve-racking and might cause you to make a very costly mistake. For example, if the price of your stock dropped consistently over time, you will probably be tempted to cut your losses and invest in a more stable company. Sometimes a drop in stock price might be caused by a temporary episode of poor earnings, a major shareholder divesting at once and flooding the market with shares, or other reasons that do not necessarily reflect a failing company. If you followed the fundamental analysis process before picking your stock, chances are that you invested in a stable and profitable company so there would really be no reason to worry. Let's say that after a month or so your share is down 30% from your purchase price. After weeks of monitoring the price you finally decide that you were wrong in your assessment and decide to sell. Six months afterwards, the stock gradually picks up and rises far above the price at which you had bought it. You just lost out on a great investment opportunity. With a portfolio, that drop in price would seem much less distressing because it would be counteracted by better performance in another asset in your portfolio.

The key function of diversifying your investment with a portfolio is to reduce the overall volatility of your investment. To become a successful investor, you will need to learn the subtle art of balancing risk and reward over the long run. It is a decision you make to invest smart and see your savings grow above market level, with dividends and your own contributions shoring up the investment over time. The alternative is to leave your money in a savings account with below-inflation level interest rates and consistently lose purchasing power.

On one end, you have the simplicity of saving for the future by opening a bank account and on the other, aggressively investing in stocks, bonds, trusts, and other assets. One is extremely conservative and grows at way below inflation; the other is very risky and jeopardizes your entire future. The midway point between these two extremes, and the path you should endeavor to follow, is smart investing. The kind of investing that recognizes the futility of saving lots of money and seeing a large portion of it go up in flames as a result of inflation. The kind that also recognizes the impracticality of putting your money in risky investments, whatever the potential for profit-making they might contain. A diversified investment portfolio is the ultimate smart move in investing.

The process is quite complicated; you will have to conduct lots of research to ensure that your portfolio is indeed diversified and you don't just pick up the most promising shares and bundle them into one portfolio that in reality does nothing to minimize your risk. In diversification, you are supposed to consider all the factors affecting asset prices. For example, having two or more stocks in the same industry exposes your portfolio to volatility in the event of the industry experiencing a slump. True diversification requires that you look out of the stock market into bonds, international stocks, commodity funds, real estate investment trusts, and exchange-traded funds. Even if your investment strategy is for the long term, shorter term investments like certificates of deposit present your portfolio with lower but assured rates of return in a year or so.

The four categories of a well-balanced portfolio should be domestic stocks (including REITs, and ETFs, which are considered high yield and high risk, especially over the short term), foreign stock (medium to high yield and medium risk), bonds (low yields and lower risk), and short-term investments (very low yields and virtually nonexistent risk). The system of allocating assets in a portfolio is critical to the overall profitability and risk of your investment over the short and long term.

An aggressive portfolio is composed of around 60% in domestic stocks, around 25% in foreign stocks, and approximately 15% in bonds. Short-term investments are virtually nonexistent. Such a portfolio generates an annual rate of return of around 9.5%. The best 20-year return would be 16.5% per year while the worst would be 2.6%. In one year, the portfolio could be up around 135% in the best case scenario and -60% in the worst case.

A growth portfolio would have slightly below 50% in domestic stocks, around 25% in bonds, 20% in foreign stocks, and 5% short-term investments. The portfolio would have an average of 9% in annual returns, with the best 20-year average coming in at around 15.3% and the worst at 3.1%. In a good year, the portfolio would be up 110% and in a bad one, -53%.

As your aversion to risk increases, your portfolio becomes more conservative. The most conservative portfolio substitutes domestic stocks for bonds as the biggest holding within the portfolio. Since bonds are less volatile and safer, the portfolio becomes even less likely to lose you money. The return on investment also reduces, but not as much as you would expect. As an example, let's make it so that your conservative portfolio contains 50% in bonds, 30% in the less risky short-term investments, 14% in domestic stocks, and 6% comprising of foreign stocks. This portfolio looks nothing like the aggressive one. Its potential is also miles away from what you get on your aggressive portfolio. You get an average annual rate of return of 6%, an annual best-case scenario return of 31% and worst-case return of -17.5%. On the 20-year estimate, the best-case scenario is a conservative 11% and a worst-case return of 2.9%.

Balancing the asset allocation gives you a portfolio with 40% in bonds, 35% in domestic stocks, 15% in international stocks, and 10% in short-term investments. The annual rate of return clocks in at 8%, with the best yearly return being 76.5% and the worst being -40%. Over 20 years, a balance portfolio gives 13.8% return in the best case scenario and 3.4% at the worst financial market situation.

The balanced and growth portfolios present an acceptable balance between risk and returns. The worst-case scenario return of our balanced portfolio is higher than the growth portfolio, clocking in at 3.4% versus 3.1%. Considering the best-case scenario, the difference between a balanced and growth portfolio is bigger (1.5%), but the chances of either of these two extremes happening are rather slim. The reality is more likely to be somewhere in between these two extremes, but the lowest levels possible in a balanced portfolio are higher than those likely to occur in a growth portfolio. A balanced portfolio is recommended if you care more about protecting your bottom line than increasing gains. A growth portfolio gives you almost the same returns, but with higher possible returns. The aggressive and conservative portfolios are too extreme to be effective, so you should probably steer clear.

Case study: The 2008 Financial Market Crash

The early 2000s were a tough few years for the U.S. economy. Minor recessions were experienced after the 2001 terrorist attacks, after the burst of the dot-com bubble, and after several major financial institutions were caught up in an accounting scandal. In a bid to stave off a recession, the Federal Reserve was forced to lower fund rates from 6.5% in 2000 to 1.75% in 2001. This created massive liquidity in the economy. Subprime borrowers could now access home loans on 100% of the value of their houses and banks, counting on the massive demand their massive loans were creating in the market, expected home prices to appreciate.

House prices did appreciate and subprime mortgages became the new investment frontier in the financial markets. Low inflation emboldened the Fed to continue slashing interest rates, bottoming out at 1% in June 2003. Cheap and readily available credit encouraged people to borrow and keep borrowing, with the subprime mortgage market especially loose in its lending terms. Bankers also unearthed a new way to make money by repackaging subprime loans into collateralized debt obligations passed on to bigger institutional bankers like Merrill Lynch, Morgan Stanley, Goldman Sachs, Bear Stearns, and Lehman Brothers. These secondary lenders could now take on massive secondary debt on subprime loans thanks to relaxed capital requirements by the SEC that allowed these banks to leverage loans up to as much as 40 times of initial investment.

Soon, the whole house of cards started to unravel. In the year 2004, home ownership had reached 70%- the highest levels ever and buyers were quickly drying up. A year later, prices were in free fall, and the U.S. Home Construction Index was down 40%. Higher interest rates imposed by the Fed sent subprime payments to the roof, leading to mass defaulting by homeowners. The first signs of serious troubles were now appearing.

In the first quarter of 2007, companies that dealt in subprime lending had started to file for bankruptcy en masse. A total of 25 had already gone under by March and more were headed that way. The media started reporting on the growing crisis, highlighting the horror stories surrounding the mass bankruptcies in the subprime market and fueling speculation on the effect the collapse on the whole financial industry.

The first real panic was felt when news reports revealed that hedge funds had invested over $1 trillion in the subprime mortgage market. If borrowers continued to default, the whole financial market would be sent into a tailspin that would take down markets all over the world. Banking institutions started fighting for survival the same way they had fought each other over the collateralized debt obligations. In June 2007, Merrill Lynch made headlines by seizing about $800 million worth of assets from hedge funds securitized by competitor Bear Stearns.

As the situation turned from bad to worse, the subprime disaster extended its reach outside the U.S. Banks have always offered each other bargain prices on loans, but now everyone wanted to protect their own backs. The Northern Rock bank, one of the biggest banks in England, found itself facing liquidity issues. The Bank of England had to step in and bail it out to avoid a market panic. The whole world was just starting to realize the extent of the subprime crisis. Governments around the world formed a task force to attempt to find an urgent solution to avert disaster.

Governments of the most affected countries committed to providing liquidity backing for financial institutions in the hope that they would rescue the interbank market (the system through which banks borrow from each other) and give the financial sector a chance to recover. Some businesses, however, were too far gone to be rescued. Lehman Brothers, one of the oldest and most influential investment banks in U.S. filed for bankruptcy. Soon afterwards, Indymacbowed to massive losses. Bear Stearns and Merrill Lynch were rescued by JP Morgan Chase and Bank of America respectively and the government took over control of Freddie Mac and Fannie Mae to prevent them facing the same fate.

At the heart of the financial crisis was American International Group (AIG), an insurance company that had taken over the insurance for subprime mortgages. The insurance coverage allowed banks, hedge funds, and other financial institutions to purchase these very risky assets with confidence. Soon, a majority of investors owned mortgage-backed securities either directly or indirectly through REITs, trust funds, or ETFs.

When the home ownership market became bloated and prices started to drop, banks and other institutional investors insured by AIG were entitled to a settlement as per the insurance terms. However, AIG was facing a cash crunch of its own and would not be able to cover all pledges. It was this failure by AIG that prompted the freeze in interbank borrowing and sent the whole financial markets into a tailspin.

The stock market is intertwined with the banking industry. Companies deposit excess funds on money market funds, with banks in turn using the cash to give short term loans. A day after the Fed advanced a bailout loan of $85 billion to AIG on September 16th, 2008, companies rushed to withdraw their monies from money market funds; a huge number put the money in safer investments like treasury bonds.

The stock market was already reeling from the shock of financial giants like Lehman Brothers collapsing. With the near-collapse of money market funds and fears of a total collapse of the economy raging, the stock market went into the worst single day downward spiral in the stock market. Republican lawmakers in Congress were opposing a proposed bill to rescue failing financial institutions- the only hope to frightened investors in the stock market- and tensions on Wall Street were running high. After an initial rejection of the bill, everything unraveled. In just a few short hours on the afternoon of September 29, investors had pulled $1.2 trillion from the stock market. The Dow fell 777.68 points, the highest ever intraday fall in its history. The bailout of the financial sector had apparently been put in place, but the stock market was still out in the cold.

From September 29, 2008 to March 5, 2009, it had dropped more than 50% to 6,594.44 in a series of searing drops as financial giants continued to close shop. Even as banks and hotshot insurer AIG continued to gobble up hundreds of billions in government bailout money, automakers started to cry out for a federal bailout. In a ravaged economy, car sales (as with every other huge expenditure) had drastically fallen in the eighteen months leading up to November 2008. It wasn't until the new Obama administration came in with an economic stimulus starting in March that things started to look up. From the lows of 6,594.44 in March, the Dow would gradually climb to 9,093.24 before going on an upwards spiral back to its initial levels and beyond. But the recovery was slow in coming and it wasn't until 2013 that the stock market could be said to have recovered fully.

For investors, the 2008 stock market crash is a scar that will not be healing soon. The widespread panic and poor performance imprinted very firmly in the minds of everyone that no giant was too big to fall. A seemingly impossible nightmare had transpired right in front of the country and things would never be the same again. Stocks like AIG, XL Group Plc, and Genworth Financial Inc. dropped up to 97%. All of these companies were in the insurance industry and had been badly exposed in the subprime mortgages fiasco.

On the other end of the spectrum, Walmart, Dollar Tree, and Amgen actually thrived during the stock market crash. These are companies that cater to the money-saving sensibilities of the American public. As the economic collapse raged through the country, their core businesses were actually boosted by the downturn. All three companies are in industries considered defensive; retail (Dollar Tree and Walmart) and healthcare (Amgen). People still needed their prescriptions and groceries, so whatever little expenditure money the public could spare went to these businesses. And while they are not exactly hot stocks in terms of dividend yield or share price growth, these defensive companies were the lifeblood of the stock market.

What should every investor learn from the 2008 stock market crash, especially from these six companies? Differentiation and diversification are indeed crucial to surviving market volatility. Few investors went through the period without losing money. Indeed, even diversified portfolios would have had a few bad apples that would have grossly affected returns, even if it contained all three thriving stocks. But if you consider that the 2008 crash was an extraordinary situation, then one lesson stands out from the noise and unprecedented losses; diversification works. Owning stocks in all three massive losers would have decimated any portfolio and wipe out an investment probably accumulated for a decade or more. But having a diversified portfolio strong on short-term investments (unaffected by the crash) and bonds (the best performers at a time when even big business was taking their cash from money market funds to buy treasury bonds) would counteract the effects of the massive declines.

Special Assets Investments

REITs

A diversified investment portfolio requires that you invest in some of the assets that are somewhat protected from the volatility of the stock market. One of the best areas to direct your investment would be a Real Estate Investment Trust (REIT), an investment vehicle that makes it possible for an individual to invest in massive real estate projects through capital pooling. REITs are offered by real estate companies who operate revenue-generating assets in the properties industry.

As an individual, it would be impossible to accumulate enough capital to invest in a mall, apartment complex, resort, or office buildings. The capital requirement is simply too high. But returns on these investments are fixed and high, especially in the long term. The risk is also minimized because REITs are administered by established companies with years of experience in properties.

Just like stocks, REITs are SEC-registered and may be bought in the bourse through stockbrokers. The options include preferred stock, debt security, and common stock, with commission charges applied.

However, some REITs are privately traded. These are called non-exchange traded REITs, which means that you cannot sell them on the floor of the stock exchange. To sell such REITs, you will need to go through the issuer, which might take a while. Buying happens through financial advisors and special brokers (non-traded REITs often target a certain demographic of the market and use stock brokers positioned to give the best access). A commission of about 10% of the investment is charged on each investment, a rather high fee that might adversely cut into your overall earnings.

It is very important that you understand this fundamental difference and its impact on your investment in a REIT before making the purchase decision. For one, it is very hard to sell non-exchange traded REITs so don't make the mistake of buying them if you want to be flexible about liquidating your investment for immediate cash rewards. Non-exchange traded REITs are also hard to value because share prices are not disclosed for the first 18 months of acquisition.

However, non-traded REITs pay handsome dividends compared to the publicly traded ones even though the lack of public scrutiny of their internal operations makes them susceptible to misappropriation. Conflicts of interest with fund managers who are hired on contract may also affect the returns and dividend yields.

REITs come in all shapes and sizes, but there are five fundamental categories; retail, residential, healthcare, office, and mortgage. Retail REITs are the most prominent of all REITs, accounting for about 25% of all combined real estate trusts. To invest in retail REITs, you will need to have a basic understanding of their operations. Look into the previous investments and look at their anchor tenants and space-letting capabilities. Earnings from a retail REIT may experience a serious plunge simply by losing an anchor tenant. Also, keep in mind that retail REITs go hand-in-hand with the retail market. Any downturn in the retail sector will cause them to underperform.

Residential REITs operate in the housing sector. They invest in and operate rental apartments especially in large cities. Other than the job market and population distribution, residential REITs are affected by little else because they cater to large market of renters in major cities like Los Angeles and New York.

Healthcare REITs have gained in prominence in the last few decades, driven by the need for healthcare facilities such as retirement homes, medical centers, hospitals, and nursing facilities. As such healthcare REITs shift in profitability with the healthcare industry. With the recent politicization of Medicaid and Medicare (the lifeblood of the healthcare industry), Healthcare REITs have become rather risky.

Office REITs cater to the office needs of the business community, relying on rents for revenue generation. The state of the economy and the startup business environment are the key considerations before buying Office REIT stock. You can expect earnings to dip when the economy declines.

Finally, mortgage REITs trade in mortgages. Debt is not just the biggest source of revenue for mortgage REITs. It is the only one. Interest rates thus have a huge effect on mortgage REITs, with increasing rates decreasing their value and decreasing interest driving their value up. However, the fact that you have zero control over interest rates as an investor makes it harder for you to profit from a mortgage REIT.

REITs are generally considered to be a high-yield asset class, with an average 20-year return of 9.9% between 1990 and 2010. Even after the real estate market precipitated the financial and stock markets crash in 2008, REITs picked up within five years to reach returns of about 10.7% between 2013 and 2016. It would be very profitable to have a REIT in your portfolio, as long as you have done your research and are assured of good returns.

International Indexes

Just like domestic index funds, international indexes represent an approximation of the value of a section of a country's stock market. Companies selected for inclusion in an international index are vetted so that their performance reflects the direction, upwards or downwards, of all sectors of the economy. International indexes fall under regional and global indexes.

Regional stock market indexes encompass stocks in certain parts of the world like the Americas, Europe, Asia, Africa, and other regions that share national boundaries. Regional indexes are a great measure of the general economic performance of a region and they also promote countries within the index as investment destinations.

Global indexes sample shares from all world countries in a particular industry or financial class. The main advantage of international indexes is that they are not constrained by national boundaries in their choice for stocks to include in the index and can most effectively offer an indication how certain sectors of the world economy are doing.

Investing in international indexes is quite challenging, because investors are conditioned to gravitate towards familiarity. The wide expanse of stocks in regional or global indexes makes it harder for you as an investor to vet each and every company in the index to determine risk. This tendency to settle for familiarity is called home bias and it is promoted by an investor's exposure to local publicity about a company so that they feel that it makes for a safer investment than a foreign company.

International indexes are great for diversification because they encompass stocks that are influenced by very diverse economic situations, a great countermeasure against volatility in local markets. In the past decade, international indexes have generated great returns of around 15%, up 10% from around 5% from the 1990s. The world has been growing more globalized in the past several decades as transaction costs and fees have consistently fallen.

Some of the most prominent international indexes include the Vanguard Developed Markets Index Fund Admiral Shares, a $102.7 billion benchmark index that tracks stock prices for the biggest companies from Canada, Europe, and the Pacific. This fund offers a 3.4% turnover ratio and requires a minimum investment of $3,000 at zero commission.

Another easy to enroll international index fund is the Schwab International Index Fund (SIIF). The index favors a more defensive bend to its stock composition and gives a 3% turnover ratio. At $1 minimum requirement, the SIIF is very accessible even for beginner investors.

Emerging markets

The U.S. stock market is one of the most active one in terms of volumes and value traded per year. As such, it is hard to find a good stock that is underpriced. Recommendations from investment gurus like Warren Buffett on value investing have turned almost every investor into an expert in finding undervalued stocks. Few have remained undervalued for more than just a couple of months. Foreign stock markets, especially in the emerging economies, present a whole other scenario. Stock undervaluation is prevalent here and with lower net incomes in native populations, investment volumes are rather low.

Yet emerging economies present great chances for investors to make good money from the stock markets as their GDPs grow at higher rates than the developed economies. In the past one year, rising interest rates have caused a correction in the stock markets of most emerging markets, leading to low prices that are granted to rise and economies grow and interest rates drop. In China, the threat of a trade war with U.S. has caused a 19.3% overall decline in the stock market while Brazil's stock has dropped 13.7% and South Korea is down 8.4%. Declining stock prices present a great buying opportunity at below market level. Furthermore, stocks in emerging marketsare valued at 50% less than those in the United States according to analysis by Pekin Hardy Strauss Wealth Management (Strauss, 2018).

Emerging markets are also growing as developed countries decline. In 1998, the United States counted for 20% of the global economy while emerging countries accounted for just 43%. Fast forward 20 years later and the emerging markets are up 16% to 59% while the U.S. has dropped to 15%. Emerging markets economies have been growing away from industry towards technology and consumer industries and as a result the middle class has been expanding exponentially.

ETFs

Exchange-Traded Funds (ETFs) are traded securities that track commodities, bonds, stock indexes, and assets. ETFs trade like stocks in the stock market, with price fluctuations throughout the trading session like stocks. ETFs are more liquid and trade at lower commission fees compared to mutual funds. In some cases, ETFs are set up as Unit Investment Trusts, which means that they will have to be recalled after a predetermined period of time. In the event of the fund being liquidated, ETFs have a residual value, slightly higher than the purchase price, which will be used to refund investors. Just like stocks, ETFs entitle investors to a dividend calculated from a portion of the profits. ETFs are traded through an exchange fund that appreciates and depreciates with demand and supply, much like the outstanding shares of a stock.

Except for a few slight differences in their basic constitutions, stocks and ETFs present the same opportunities, risks, liquidity, and tax implications. Transactions on both assets are trade-based, but stocks are generally liquid while some ETFs are harder to liquidate. While you build a stock portfolio by putting together a list of stocks, the ETF comes in its own mini-portfolio, which means that it is less volatile. Both stocks and ETFs are taxed on capital gains like any other investment. While stocks present you will thousands of options to enter a certain industry, ETFs are packaged to cover a certain sector, giving you a better opportunity to capitalize on a certain sector of the economy.

As you can see, index funds and ETFs present the best investment opportunity for an investor; one because they carry less risk, two because they are more consolidated and thus less volatile, and three because returns are more assured than with stocks. An individual stock is definitely less profitable than an ETF or index fund, but a stock portfolio allows you to hedge your bets and catch up on the benefits offered by the former.

Chapter 8: How to Profitably Select Individual Stocks

You have learned all there is to learn about investing as a beginner, including diversifying your investments to reduce volatility and increase returns over the long term. In this chapter, we will look at the most important process of becoming a stock investor, selecting the stocks to invest in.

The first rule of investing states; you should only invest in companies whose business you understand. Can you explain what a company does in 2 minutes to a 10 year old? Only when you are confident that you understand fully what a business does should you consider putting your money in it. Companies that you understand are safer because your prior understanding of it and its products or services contributes to the research you do to determine whether a company's core business is stable enough to invest in for the long run.

A company's stock can only be as successful as the product or service that puts it in the stock market. Share prices tend to drop when a company releases a product perceived as being inferior because investors expect the market to hate it and refuse to buy, which is likely to create price volatility. A perfect example of such a company is McDonalds. The business model at McDonalds is simple enough; tasty food as fast as you need it.

While insider trading is a crime under federal law, if you work in a particular industry and you have noticed that a certain company has a great product, you can use this information to position yourself for profit-making in the future. Avoid ambiguous stocks because it is the stock that you don't know that loses you money. Sometimes what appears to be a great stock turns out to be a risky investment. For example, some new pharmaceutical companies enter the market with great buzz, counting on it to launch a new drug. In the event that the IPO does not pan out, such companies fade into the background, leaving your portfolio bleeding.

Another important rule is to distribute your stock portfolio over a couple of stocks. Even if you understand a particular market or industry perfectly, pick the strongest stock of the lot and add it to other great stocks from other sectors.

Some investors maintain that past results do not guarantee great performance in the future. But past results often influence the future performance because it shapes investors' opinions about a stock. Previous performance in the stock market should count in your decision to pick a stock for your starter portfolio. The safest bet is for you to only buy stocks with a great track record of generating earnings for investors. Companies with growth patterns going back a few years to a few decades are often the strongest investment because chances of you losing money are minimal.

It has been stated before, but it bears repeating. Do not buy stocks in companies that do not give dividends. A dividend presents you with a return that you can either use to expand your holdings in the same company through DRIP or by going to a stockbroker. A dividend is money you are entitled to as a shareholder for providing the company with capital.

Finally, you should stick to those companies that are at the lead of their industry. These companies dominate and most often than not overshadow the rest of the players. To maintain their position at the front, first-rate companies innovate and disrupt the industry, always consolidating their position at the lead and generating massive returns for shareholders. The brand is also an important aspect of a business. Stocks with recognizable brands tend to outdo their counterparts in the stock market by a comfortable margin.

What should a starter stock portfolio look like?

A starter portfolio is meant to introduce you to the world of stock market investing. Starting with a portfolio straight out, instead of starting to invest before consolidating all assets in one portfolio, is a great idea because you get to decide what arrangement to use in allocating stocks to the portfolio.

The most important consideration for a starter stock portfolio is that it should be priced right. You are buying for the long run, so the lesser the purchase price of your stock, the more your investment will appreciate. The best idea to get a fair price is to go for undervalued shares; buy them cheap and watch their price rise and your investment grow. While it has been established that timing the market never works, you should only buy a stock at the lowest price at any one time. Even as you inject your monthly or annual contribution into the portfolio, do not be afraid to buy immediately after bad news when the share plummets for a while before picking up.

The performance of a business in its core activity influences the stock market in a huge way. A company that registers steadily growing revenues over a few years will see its stock price rise steadily, driven by investor confidence. Rising revenues indicate that a business remains in good financial health and is unlikely to collapse any time soon. For dividend paying stocks, the revenue growth also affects the dividend yield per share. A company that grows from year to year is likely to reward shareholders better than one that has stagnated. Before buying a company's stock, check the trend in the past 5-10 years. Only buy if there are no red flags. Otherwise, you should steer clear.

A strong market position enables a company to compete. From product distribution to publicity and brand image, the presence of a company in the market shapes investor's perception of its future stock prospects. Ensure that the company you are buying to put in your stock portfolio commands a sizeable portion of the market as this ensures that new products or services released will always perform well.

Dividends are the bread and butter of a long-term investor. The value added to the portfolio by the dividends reinvested (using a DRIP) into the company makes all the difference in the long run. If the company does not yet offer a dividend, then it is not suited for your ambitious investment plan.

What is the strategic outlook of the company you are about to buy a stake in? You can tell the strategic research and development outlook, market plans, acquisitions, among others. Not only should a portfolio stock have a definite plan for sustainable growth, these plans should be credible enough to inspire you to invest in the company.

To find the companies that will form part of your portfolio, you have to be ready to dive into the financial sections of the newspaper, research massively online, browse through financial websites, and read through boring financial report to ascertain the suitability of a company for your stock portfolio. Be sure to dig deep in your research; that is the only way you will find the companies that fit the bill for a long-term dividend stock. Sexy stocks and sexy investment opportunities in general, have a tendency to end badly. In fact, pick the most boring and predictable companies to invest in. This predictability is often in profit-making and the boring business engagements produce reliable profits, dividend yields, and stock growths even over twenty years.

Some of the most boring companies that have consistently performed brilliantly include Procter & Gamble, General Electric, The Dollar Tree, among others. The conservative nature of business growth in these companies has ensured that the expansion process remained manageable and the core business remained intact. The steady diversification of a company like General Electric has kept it relevant and dependable enough that even while facing the serious financial straits the company has been going through, it has remained a very popular stock in the stock market.

You should never buy or sell stocks based on mainstream media reporting. Instead, let your fundamental evaluation of a company inform your actions, whether buying or selling. If you are hoping to take advantage of the great potential of value investing you should especially turn a blind ear because value investing calls for buying while everyone else is selling. Neither should you listen to your friends' speculation about the bright future of this or that company, unless your friend is Warren Buffett. All these forms of investing (from media reporting to a friend's recommendation) qualify as reactionary investing. And you might just as well spend all your money or put it in a savings account, because you will lose it in the long run when you engage in reactionary investing.

Starter Portfolio Stocks

Berkshire Hathaway

Berkshire Hathaway is the $203 billion investment vehicle of world's richest investor Warren Buffett. The company started as a textile manufacturer, but its claim to fame has been as one of the biggest investment companies the world over, with stakes in a hundreds of listed companies. Under Warren Buffett, Berkshire has accumulated a portfolio of forever businesses in banking, insurance, furniture, retail, and numerous other long-term investments.

But with Berkshire Hathaway, you will be assured of not just a great return on your investment, but also a very fundamentally strong stock. The company is organized like a huge portfolio with carefully picked stocks, so market volatility is very low. Moreover, Berkshire is one of those defensive stocks that thrive through tough economic conditions, even when its constituent stocks falter.

Unlike other companies with a celebrity manager at the head, Berkshire has a well-established line of succession. Ted Weschler and Todd Combs, two of Warren's senior most managers, have proven themselves to be quite adept at picking stocks to invest in. They are also well recognized in the industry, so no one will be liquidating their shares when Warren Buffett is no longer in charge.

McDonald's

As a prospective starter portfolio stock pick, McDonald's gives the dividend and stock price growth combo that is quite rare and extremely valuable for you as a long term investor. A financially conservative approach to doing business has ensured that McDonald's does not pull any overambitious stunts to win market share, the one issue that plagues many good companies and drives them to make suicide moves. Instead, a well thought-out long-term growth strategy moderates its business practices.

As a listed company in the Good Business Portfolio, McDonald's has exploded in growth in the past three years after flat lining in the previous two. And it has not been just a slight bump, but steady, sustainable growth in stock prices as dividend rates increased and earnings results improved every year.

Even though the company grows at a much slower rate compared to some stocks in the market, the rate of growth is high enough to make it one of those invest-and-forget companies. A 2.4% dividend yield is also a great motive for investing in McDonald's for the benefit of those dividend reinvestments to further bolster your portfolio.

Disney

In chapter 5, we analyzed Disney as a dividend stock. While it remains a low-dividend paying company, Disney has been growing its dividend payout over the last couple of years and with outstanding future prospects, that payout is likely to just keep climbing. So, Disney qualifies as a great portfolio pick on account of its attractiveness as a dividend stock with even greater dividend potential.

The price itself is another reason to buy Disney stock. Between 2005 and 2019, the share price rose $111 from $24. That is a 460% appreciation in initial investment in 14 years. At a current valuation of $250 billion, Disney is either undervalued or overvalued depending on the financial tool you use to calculate its valuation. By discounted cash flow (DCF), it is 28% overvalued. But with relative valuation tools, you will find that Disney is undervalued by about 3.5%. But as a dividend stock with a stock price that has been rising consistently in the last 14 years, Disney is an all-round great pick as a starter portfolio stock.

Coca-Cola

Coca-Cola is without doubt one of the most recognizable brands in the world of beverage right now. It also has the best market penetration of any beverage company, selling in almost every single country in the world. The share has been growing at an average of 11.5% over the past 10 years. Even though this rate of growth is low by S&P 500 standards, it is still an attractive return.

Coca-Cola is a dividend stock, with a 3.1% yield in 2018. At 67% of net incomes, the company still has a lot of money in its coffers to continue developing new beverage flavors, like the Orange Vanilla Coke launched in 2019. This new flavor adds to an impressive array of options in cold drinks, fruit juices, bottled water, and energy drinks- diversification without moving out of the scope of the core business for which the company has established itself. Another reason why you should invest in Coca-Cola is that you will be joining Berkshire Hathaway in the shareholders register. Need I say more?

General Electric

General Electric is one of those legacy companies that have been around for so long that it has become part of the American corporate mainstay. Even though the stock plummeted terribly after the 2009 financial crisis, it has been making steady progress in the last few years.

Its core business is still thriving, debts are well under control, and the issue of leadership has seemingly been resolved with the recent appointment of Lawrence Culp as CEO and Chairman. Culp's apparent willingness to make the hard choices previous inbred CEOs were unwilling to make has put GE well on the path to recovery. If the share price continues rising at the current rate of 35% every quarter, then the low prices the stock is trading at present a massive buying opportunity.

While GE historically awarded great dividend to its shareholders, its dividend rates are currently rather disappointing as the company faces a downturn in its financial performance. GE will not reward you with handsome dividends any time soon. But if you are willing to hold on to the stock for the price, buying it at the current rock-bottom price of under $10 will guarantee you great profits when the stock returns to its previous highs of over $30.

UPS

United Parcel Service Inc. is mail and packages delivery business that operates around the world. With a fleet of cargo planes and delivery vans and trucks to rival that of market leader FedEx, UPS has continued to exert its dominance in the parcels delivery business. UPS has been growing its market share consistently over time by opening up new markets, strengthening its standing as a beginner stock portfolio stock with huge potential for growth.

The stock is one of the most dependable dividend paying shares in the stock market. The company has consistently performed above and beyond market expectations over a long time.

In 2018, UPS ramped up its bottom line by 52%, achieving record-setting earnings growth and a mind-blowing 174% return on share price.

Walmart

Walmart is a great stock to add to your portfolio for a number of reasons, chief among which is the fact that as a brand, the business remains strong in its brick-and-mortar stores even as the online sales have risen gradually. E-commerce is the reason why Walmart lost the pole position to Amazon, but double digit growth in online sales promise to give the company at least a chance to challenge Amazon's newfound dominance.

Until Amazon waltzed in and ruined the party, Walmart was the largest retail company in U.S. Even though online sales and changing consumer preferences have been changing consumer behavior to the detriment of Walmart, the company remains strong financially, reporting store sales growth of 3.4% in 2018, even as it makes moves to enter the online sales space.

Walmart is a defensive stock from a strong company you can count on to be around for a long time, adapting to market changes to continue offering great value for you investment going forward.

JP Morgan Chase

Founded over 200 years ago, JP Morgan Chase is without doubt one of the oldest investment banks in America. The bank has also grown to become one of the biggest in the world with assets totaling over $2.6 trillion as of 2018.

There are quite a few reasons to buy and retain JP Morgan in your stock portfolio. First is the long history of profitable growth. The company is well established as a banking giant, a leader in lending, investment financing, credit cards, and a myriad of other financial services. Moreover, the company's stock offers good dividend payout at 2.9%. over the long terms JPM has been increasing dividend yields at the rate of as high as 42%.

JP Morgan also stands out from the rest of the banking industry by the defensive nature of its stock. Even during the 2008 stock market crash when financial institutions were declaring bankruptcy and falling to zero share price, JP Morgan remained strong enough to buy out some of the poor performers.

Looking for faster returns? Check out these high potential stocks

Facebook

Facebook is one of the four tech companies that make up the FANG (Facebook, Amazon, Netflix, and Google) group of high performing stocks. Facebook is one of the more controversial social media companies, widely criticized in the run-up to the 2016 general election for selling user data. Despite the criticism, Facebook has continued to outperform market expectations, raising massive revenues from advertising, its main source of revenue. Facebook has been investing in growth areas, opening new revenue sources every year to bolster its standing in the market. These new avenues generate massive value for shareholders.

Even though the price of Facebook stock has been rising consistently since its 2012 IPO, it remains to be an undervalued stock with massive value investment opportunity. The stock has a P/E ratio of 42.1 which is much lower than the 70% average earnings growth rate. Facebook will remain undervalued at its current earnings levels until the share hits $288.

Netflix

Netflix has come to disrupt the movie and television industries with its online video streaming services. The company has managed to disrupt one of the oldest, most conservative industries of the 20th century and is currently riding the internet wave to glorious success in financial earnings and market share. The price of Netflix fluctuates around the $400 mark and even though the stock does not offer dividends (few tech companies do), you can be assured of great rewards in the future. The current high subscription rates hint at a very profitable future for the company.

Over the long term, the world looks to be heading towards greater internet penetration, meaning that internet-based companies will dominate. Even then, only 10% of the market has been penetrated, which means that the company is yet to come by even greater financial success as internet television gains popularity outside the U.S.

Amazon

There are many reasons to put Amazon in your stock portfolio as a growth stock. First off, the company is hugely successful, commanding 50% of the U.S. e-commerce market in 2018. A year before, the company only had 44% of that market. Amazon is remarkable for this kind of surges.

Just when you think it has reached the ceiling, Amazon goes ahead and proves you wrong by doing even better.

And while the online shopping division of Amazon is more popular, the company also has a cloud computing unit that has been causing waves in cloud infrastructure. Amazon currently commands 35% of this sector, beating out veteran giants like IBM, Microsoft, Alibaba, and Google.

As of now, Amazon's book value stands at just above $350 billion, but its market cap is much higher, having exceeded $1 trillion once. It could very easily reach this capitalization sometime in the future and you'd be well advised to position yourself to profit from that possibility by buying into the company now.

Skyworks

Skyworks is one of the largest semiconductors manufacturers in the U.S. One of Skyworks' biggest clients is Apple and the company (and thus its stock) has suffered quite a lot of volatility from this partnership. The stock is currently undergoing a downturn and has plummeted to levels it had sunk to in 2015 after Apple went through a sales slump on its smart phones. However, in other metric Skyworks remains stronger than ever, with future prospects actually quite rosy. Skyworks will be launching its 5G microchips in the next year or so, with sales expected to be meteoric.

By the principles of value investing, Skyworks is a stock that has received a beating from overblown negative publicity surrounding uncertainty over sales for the upcoming Apple smartphones. This could be the opportunity of a lifetime to buy a stock that has a very good chance of doing very well. Another reassuring fact is that Skyworks currently has plans to diversify from Apple smart phone chips, meaning that its stock will soon gain more autonomy.

Baidu

Over the past 10 years, Baidu is one of the world's best performing stocks. Since 2009, the share price has shot up over 1,200%- a mind-blowing appreciation in value for initial investors. Baidu is considered the Google of China, enjoying virtually unchallenged dominance of the search engine market. As the company expands into artificial intelligence and cloud storage, it is opening up new grounds for dominance and sources of revenue. The massive Chinese market makes Baidu's growth space quite substantial, which means that its revenues and stock prices might rise yet higher. However, you will have to contend with the Chinese government and its rather interfering ways in regard to cyberspace.

Even with its 1,200% rise in stock price, Baidu remains cheaply priced, with its P/E ratio being a measly 0.2, which indicates that shareholders are still buying the company's stock at bargain price. A value investment in a company with a record of 1,200% rise in stock price could be very profitable in the future.

Okta

Okta is a cloud computing company that provides software-as-a-service products for businesses. Buying Okta now gives you the opportunity to own a stake in the company at considerably lower prices. If it follows the trend of other tech companies, the stock will be up higher than the current 132% since its IPO in just a couple of years and much higher in the long term. Current financial reporting from the company indicates revenue growths of up to 57% against projections of around 40%. A company that beats its own revenue projections is always a worthwhile investment.

Another area where Okta has outdone itself is in attracting huge customers. So far, the company can boast of Nordstrom, JetBlue, BOK Financial, and 21st Century Fox as part of its customer base. And even though the company is still a loss reader spending more money in investment equity than it makes as it seeks to break even, its future prospects still make it a strong growth stock.

Prudential Financial

Prudential Financial is easily the world's biggest life insurance company, but it is also a diversified financial services company with business interests in pensions, international markets, and retirement benefits. The company's stocks have been growing consistently over the last few years- 10% on average- with future projections pegged at 8.5%. As a financial company, prudential does better in times of economic expansion like right now. Its upwards growth is also supported by rising premiums in life insurance premiums and growing world economy. Japan is one international market that the company has been reaping great profits from in the past few years and this trend is only expected to rise as premiums rise towards $1 trillion in that particular market.

Another reason why Prudential's huge growth potential is so encouraging is the fact that the company is over 140 years old. It is the oldest of all the growth stocks listed in this section. Age is very reassuring for stock investing.

Garmin

Garmin is a diversified IoT products company that came up with fitness app Fitbit among other applications. With sales rising more than 50% every year for the last three years, Garmin has become one of the most profitable wearable tech companies.

Garmin is particularly attractive as a growth portfolio stock because it gives dividends at around 2.5% yield, with increases in dividend payout increased by up to 16% in 2018.

Conclusion – The 7 Golden Investment Rules for Long-Term Profitability and Life-Long Financial Prosperity

If you are to take anything from this book, let these 7 golden rules of investing be it. If you follow these rules to the letter, you can be assured of meeting your investment goals with minimal risk.

There is a big difference between investing and trading. As an investor, your decision to buy into a company is informed by the long-term prospects of its stock. Buying a stock to sell in the short term makes you a trader and a trader is just someone who speculates on markets much like gamblers speculate on the outcome of a football match.

1. Do not consider stocks that do not pay dividends. The dividend is your reward for investing in a company and it is the most important aspect of stock market investing. Studies have shown that reinvested dividends remarkably increase the yields from an investment portfolio. A stock with dividends produces up to 20 times the yields of a similarly priced stock with no dividends after 20 years of reinvestment. If a stock doesn't pay dividends and the only way for you to make money is to wait until the price rises to an acceptable level and then sell, then that is a speculation. Moreover, the stock price will be more volatile because it now relies on future rather than current prospects.

2. Smart investors use the principles of dollar-cost averaging to improve their chances of success at an investment. Dollar-cost averaging allows you to buy shares at the fairest possible price by buying multiple times at different prices. By following dollar-cost averaging to buy assets for long-term investment, not only do you get into the whole bargain-buying frame of mind, you are also assured of higher overall incomes in the future.

3. Buy stocks that are undervalued by going against the market as long as you are sure of a company's underlying strength. This rule follows Warren Buffett's own stated principle; *be fearful when everyone else is being greedy and be greedy when the rest of the market is fearful.* And while we are at it, don't just rely on the mainstream media for your buy/sell decision, okay?

4. It is impossible to be 100% sure of making money from an investment of just one kind.

Risk is a reality every investor has to face up to. But risks need not translate into losses if you cover your back properly. Diversification is the most effective way to ensure that your investment will not take you into the red sections of your balance sheet. You should be diligent enough to scour the market for different types of assets like ETFs, REITS, bonds, international indexes, etc to include in your portfolio. Diversification reduces the volatility of any one investment and significantly boosts your chances of seeing a great return at the end of 20 years.

5. Be very very wary of bubbles. Any asset or commodity that experiences inexplicable price surges driven by massive speculation my investors should be a no-no. Not even the temptation of being the early investor who cashes out before the bubble bursts and prices plummet should tempt you to invest in a "hot" asset/commodity. With no sure ceiling price at which you can sell, bubbles often burst earlier than expected, leading to massive losses even for the "smart" early investors.

6. The last rule is also the most important. When investing in the stock market, keep in mind that you are really investing in individual companies, so pick them very carefully. Boring is safe and defensive where bold is risky but likely to be more profitable over time. You should perform your homework about a company very carefully; understand their business operations, future prospects, and for the love of God, do buy an IPO. The initial euphoria over the company makes it very hard to determine future prospects.

Stock Market Investing for Beginners

The Top 101 Growth Stocks for 2019 – Including Marijuana Stocks, 5G Stocks, Penny Stocks and Dividends + How to Build a Starter Portfolio for Less than $100

Written By

Everyman Investing

Introduction

So you want to make a million dollars in the stock market? Is that possible and if it is, how does one accomplish it? Well, to answer both of those questions yes it is possible and there are many ways to accomplish it. For sure, it is easier if you have six figures to invest, but what if you only have five, four, or even three to get the job done? Yes, it can still be done with the right strategy and patience. It does not happen overnight and can take many years of up and down roller coaster riding to accomplish your goals. So you need to be prepared to choose the right stocks, leave your money in them, and watch the market religiously.

I am not talking about becoming a day trader watching a screen all day or someone chained to the stock market scroll, but just being someone that is aware of how trends affect companies and when to move or hold your position based on those. The best strategy is one where you do all of the research and leg work up front and then simply "lock and load" when it comes time to invest. That strategy is to pick the best growth stocks, invest early, and let your money grow with the stock. How do you pick those? By becoming aware of current business trends and growth industries from which the best growth stocks will come.

This book will give you the blueprint to choose from over 100 of them, starting for $100 or less. You will learn their industries, and be aware of how trends may change them in the future. The key to achieving financial freedom is to learn to spot those winners, invest, and hold. So, if you are ready to become a junior analyst and a wise investor, read on.

Chapter One: Growth Stocks

What are Growth Stocks? Well, in short, they are companies that grow higher than the market average. In addition, they do not give out dividends (or payments back to the stockholders for profits and growth each quarter) but instead, invest those back into the business to keep growing. When compared with traditional or Blue Chip stocks that pay those dividends, it can seem like a speculative or risky investment. However, what you must realize is that earnings from the rising stock price are usually more long term and outpace what might have come from a dividend. These stocks are usually tied to the hot growth industries which carry current biotech, marijuana, cloud technology, AI, 5G cellular, and nanotechnology. Their price on the exchange is considered their actual value no matter how high the price and you earn profits from the steady growth of the exchange price over a period of at least five years. Think of the appreciation of the price of a house or luxury car. It is much the same here, all profits are capital gains based on the resale of the stock. Very simple no muss no fuss and no complicated algorithms.

Here are some simple methods for picking Growth Stocks per Stockpicking.com

- Strong historical earnings growth. Companies should show a track record of strong earnings growth over the previous 5 to 10 years. The general idea is that if the company has displayed good growth in the recent past, it's likely to continue doing so moving forward.

- Strong forward earnings growth. Watch out for the release of the company's earnings reports (required by law for public corporations). This is an official public statement of a company's profitability for a specific period – typically a quarter or a year. These announcements are made on specific dates usually according to the quarter system and are linked to estimates that are issued by analysts. If it shows better than average or at least average growth, the stock is a good bet.

- Strong profit margins. A company's profit is calculated by deducting all expenses from sales (barring taxes) and dividing by sales. It's an important metric to consider because a company can have fantastic growth in sales but poor profit margins. This would mean that the upper management is not great at controlling costs in relation to revenues. If a company exceeds its previous five-year average of pretax profit margins – as well as those of its industry – the company may be a good growth candidate.

- Strong return on equity. The return on equity (ROE) measures its profit margin based on the money shareholders have invested. It's calculated by dividing net income by shareholder equity. Stable or increasing ROE indicates that management is doing a good job generating returns from shareholders' investments or money borrowed and is operating the business efficiently.

- Strong stock performance. In general, if a stock cannot realistically double in five years, **it's probably not a growth stock**. Keep in mind, a stock's price would double in seven years with a growth rate of just 10%. To double in five years, the growth rate must be 15%. But really it is much simpler, if you don't see growths of double, don't bother.

Ask a broker, a member of management, or yourself the following:

(Source: investopedia.com)

Question 1: *Where do you see sales trending in the next 12 to 24 months?*

A longer time period will give the investor a good glimpse of the opportunities and the risks that could present themselves over both the short and intermediate-term. Make sure you keep watch on the stock for an extended period.

Question 2: *What are the risks associated with the sourcing of raw material, or holding the line on costs of services?*

By asking this question, you will be able to learn whether there are any potential difficulties for the company in terms of acquiring raw materials or labor in the future. This can give you an idea of how the company's profit may change in the intermediate and long-term.

Question 3: *What is the best use for the cash on the company's balance sheet?*

This question will indicate whether the company is planning a large scale expansion or merger. It will also indicate whether or not they are a conservative type of management or are more interested in how they are perceived. Look for a response that would key in on whether the company is taking steps to improve its place in the market. If the company isn't growing and is losing cash, then you know what kind of performance to expect.

Question 4: *Who are the emerging competitors in the industry in which you operate?*

This question will let indicate whether they know who to watch out for and they're up against. It may also let you know of unknown rivals that may be coming to market, which could impact the company at some point down the road. Consequently, management may also disclose how it plans to deal with its new or existing competitors all together

Question 5: *What part or aspect of the business is giving you the most trouble now?*

The answer will show weaknesses in the company's organization and provide some insight into future earnings. For example, if the manager indicates that one or more sections or divisions were unprofitable or too expensive to operate this will give you a good indication that there is a hole that needs to be plugged. Identifying problem areas is just one part of the equation. It is far more important to hear about solutions to the problem.

Question 6: *How close is Wall Street in terms of estimating your company's earnings results?*

With this question, you're asking if the company will meet or beat the street's estimate. If the manager indicates that they are always under or even overestimated by analysts then it could be an indication that the "street" is off on this company and that could be problematic.

Question 7: *What part of the business do you think is being ignored that has more upside potential than Wall Street is giving it?*

This question will show the managers passion. That could be an indicator that he/she or the entire management team has a positive outlook on the business. If they do not then that is a huge problem in itself. However, if they are overconfident in the face of contrary evidence, this could be a sign that they will run an unsubstantiated "maverick" strategy that in a solid company can be a huge advantage, but in a problem company can lead to ruin.

Question 8: *Do you have any plans to advance or promote the stock?*

Knowing whether management plans to promote the stock to all investors is a sign that either they believe in themselves or they don't. The savvy investor can buy into the stock ahead of what could be a large amount of buying pressure.

Question 9: *What catalysts will affect the stock going forward?*

The manager is likely to give the investor a wealth of information. This is due to the fact people like to talk about both their and their company's accomplishments. Whether or not they speak the facts will let you know what the future outlook will be. Including investment information about negative catalysts that could adversely impact the share price.

Growth Industries

No investment strategy suits every type of person all the time. This is particularly true for young Millennial and Generation Z investors. However, identifying growth stocks and industries is always a wise bet. As such, high-growth stocks are ideal for both young-adult and novice investors. Most young investors have 80% of their portfolio in stocks, and the remainder in safer, interest-yielding assets. Time is money and the extra time allows riskier investments to expand to their full potential. With the Bull Market we are experiencing, now is a perfect chance to take advantage of longer-term growth forecasts.

Whenever discussions about high-growth stocks arise, one must talk about e-commerce and how it overwhelmingly dominates the retail sector. Remember the newer generation has grown up in a time without the brick-and-mortar hegemony and thus is more inclined to participate in the e-commerce sector.

Considering that young people do nearly everything online, e-commerce companies that sell unorthodox items and charge a premium for them are the wave of the future. In addition, the fact that half of the US workforce will be independent contractors by 2020 also means that apps and companies intended to help with that transition will be a huge source of growth. For those of you who have worked in Fortune 500 or 100 companies, you have seen the intensity of big organizations. They need help to handle the needs of tens of thousands of workers and they need unified platforms to help find both employees and contractors.

Another factor is that by the time Millennials are looking at retirement, marijuana will have likely become legal. In fact, rumors are it may be legalized nationwide by 2020. Just as the Prohibition Era failed to curb Americans' desire for alcohol, the current period will fail to reduce people's desire for cannabis. This is in addition to the numerous beneficial uses of its derivatives. It's only a matter of time before the government listens to the will of the people. When that day comes, companies dealing in marijuana such as Cannabis Growth Corporation will exponentially rise in value.

Next, as more people are cashless and paying for things card-free with apps, any payment processor will be a great growth stock.

The world of virtual living and having everything in the home on a "smart system" is the next big thing. So, investing in companies that produce wireless and AI related products is a boon. Experts forecast that by the year 2020, home automation will become a $50 billion industry.

1.Biotech-In layman's terms is the process of combining biological elements with synthetic elements to produce a molecular change and a whole new product or function from the originals. This is what the companies that make up this sector do. The sector is divided into four different categories of companies. Those that make products for healthcare, agriculture/food, industrial (chemicals for cleaning and non-edible function including environmentally friendly products), fuel, land preservation, and warfare. The Biotech Industry is divided into many different subcategories based on the sub-sector they serve:

A. Gold Biotech - these are companies that use computer components and mechanics to affect biological issues-such as pharma and medical technologies for surgery or treatment.

B. Blue Biotech - this centers on the use of sea algae to create new sources of fuel.

C. Green Biotech - these companies focus on agriculture and genetic manipulation of seeds and waste/pest reduction.

D. Red Biotech - companies focusing on genetic engineering for disease prevention like stem cells.

E. White Biotech - focuses on new chemicals or enzymes that can make the manufacturing process cheaper and faster.

F. Yellow Biotech - focuses on food production and new genetic strains of food crops.

G. Gray Biotech - focuses on the preservation of ecological diversity and lowering levels of pollution.

H. Brown Biotech - these companies focus on rehabilitating arid areas like desserts to make them capable of supporting life.

I. Violet Biotech - focuses on using technology to solve social issues.

J. Dark Biotech - focuses on the darker side of Biotech such as chemical and biological weapons.

2.Marijuana - Companies that make up the thriving and new cannabis industry comprise this grouping. They don't just cover the growth, harvest, production, and sale of the actual plant, but also things like cannabis oil products and various ingestion tools (bongs, pipes, and e-cigs). In addition, things made from byproducts of the plant like hemp fabric, fuel (can cross over into biotech), and hemp protein food products. Cannabis was first legalized in Uruguay in 2013 and Canada in 2018, with many other countries discussing it. As for the USA, the states vary (as shown in the below chart from Map of Marijuana).

State	Legal Status	Medicinal	Decriminalized
Alabama	Fully Illegal	No	No
Alaska	Fully Legal	Yes	Yes
Arizona	Mixed	Yes	No
Arkansas	Mixed	Yes	No
California	Fully Legal	Yes	Yes
Colorado	Fully Legal	Yes	Yes
Connecticut	Mixed	Yes	Reduced
Delaware	Mixed	Yes	Reduced
District of Columbia	Fully Legal	Yes	Yes

Florida	Mixed	Yes	No
Georgia	Mixed	Yes	No
Hawaii	Mixed	Yes	No
Idaho	Fully Illegal	No	No
Illinois	Mixed	Yes	Reduced
Indiana	Fully Illegal	No	No
Iowa	Fully Illegal	No	No
Kansas	Fully Illegal	No	No
Kentucky	Fully Illegal	No	No
Louisiana	Mixed	Yes	No
Maine	Fully Legal	Yes	Yes
Maryland	Mixed	Yes	Reduced
Massachusetts	Fully Legal	Yes	Yes
Michigan	Fully Legal	Yes	Yes

Minnesota	Mixed	Yes	Reduced
Mississippi	Fully Illegal	No	Reduced
Missouri	Mixed	Yes	Reduced
Montana	Mixed	Yes	No
Nebraska	Fully Illegal	No	Reduced
Nevada	Fully Legal	Yes	Yes
New Hampshire	Mixed	Yes	Reduced
New Jersey	Mixed	Yes	No
New Mexico	Mixed	Yes	Reduced
New York	Mixed	Yes	Reduced
North Carolina	Fully Illegal	No	Reduced
North Dakota	Mixed	Yes	No
Ohio	Mixed	Yes	Reduced
Oklahoma	Mixed	Yes	No

Oregon	Fully Legal	Yes	Yes
Pennsylvania	Mixed	Yes	No
Rhode Island	Mixed	Yes	Reduced
South Carolina	Fully Illegal	No	No
South Dakota	Fully Illegal	No	No
Tennessee	Fully Illegal	No	No
Texas	Fully Illegal	No	No
Utah	Mixed	Yes	No
Vermont	Fully Legal	Yes	Yes
Virginia	Fully Illegal	No	No
Washington	Fully Legal	Yes	Yes
West Virginia	Mixed	Yes	No
Wisconsin	Fully Illegal	No	No
Wyoming	Fully Illegal	No	No

As you may guess this is still rather volatile as it is not fully legal in the USA and has only just started on the international front, but the outlook is bright with news that North American sales of cannabis and related products topped 6.7 billion in 2016. Colorado and California alone generated 226 million and 345 million, respectively, in additional taxes during the tax year 2018. These numbers have been increasing by a rate of 30% every year in both sales and taxes. It is evident that both the private and public sector already see the potential to generate money with marijuana and that full legalization is on the distant horizon.

In addition, the sale of non-Tetrahydrocannabinol (THC-the enzyme that produces the high in marijuana) marijuana is readily available in all 50 states and in many countries in which the full substance is still illegal. Revenue from the sale of these products is expected to hit 22 billion by 2022. Edibles and oils made with Cannabis oil have been cited as an essential oil and are considered very beneficial in treating things like:

1. Anxiety/depression-initial tests in animals and humans show that applying the oil can calm panic attacks and help prevent them.

2. Pain-the anti-inflammatory properties of the oil have been shown to help reduce chronic pain by up to 15% in humans.

3. Heart Health-initial testing reveals that the application of a few drops has been able to reduce the inflammation that can contribute to cardiovascular events.

4. Nausea-it has been shown that the oil can help reduce feelings of uneasiness and nausea by 9%.

5. Skin Ailments-the oil is undergoing studies that show it may help reduce skin irritation and clear acne.

6. Antipsychotic Effects-studies suggest that CBD may help people by reducing psychotic symptoms.

7. Substance Abuse Treatment-CBD has been shown to modify circuits in the brain related to drug addiction and reduce substance dependence.

8. Anti-tumor Effects-in test-tube and animal studies CBD has demonstrated that it can slow the spread of breast, prostate, brain, colon and lung cancer.

9. Diabetes Prevention-in mice it reduced the incidence/symptoms of diabetes by 56%.

Source Healthline.com

The uses of the related Cannabis Plant Protein called Hemp are also a source of great economic and societal boons as we are discovering more and more about it. Sales of Hemp products are estimated to be at 2.6 Billion by 2022 and cover a variety of markets and uses like:

1. Pet Food-the protein has shown great promise in the production of animal feed by using the heavy and easily digestible protein in pet food, especially for those with sensitive stomachs.

2. Human Food-the protein can make a variety of things for human consumption as it is full of amino acids. Vegan and vegetarian products like powders and faux meats are already made of hemp and things like salad dressings, cooking oils, and flour can be made from the seeds.

3. Fabric-hemp has been shown to be capable of being made into sturdy fabrics to produce clothes/bedding/industrial materials.

4. Oil Bases-hemp seed oil can be reduced to a pure oil to serve as a lubricant for industrial use and as a base for consumer products like lotions.

5. Fuel-the fuel industry has long been doing research on the use of hemp as a fossil fuel alternative. Currently, it's being used in biodiesel and ethanol.

6. Paper-paper made from hemp is of high quality and the production of hemp is much easier and take up less space than other paper/food producing plants.

7. Concrete-hemp particles can provide the base for a form of cement that is just as strong as other types. It is currently being used in home construction.

Source: cannabis reports

The sale of Marijuana-Related accessories and products has already topped 20 million per year in the USA alone, so it is also a booming market. The breakdown of products is shown below from Marijuana Business Daily.

Cannabis Entrepreneurs' Outlook For The Next 12 Months By Sector

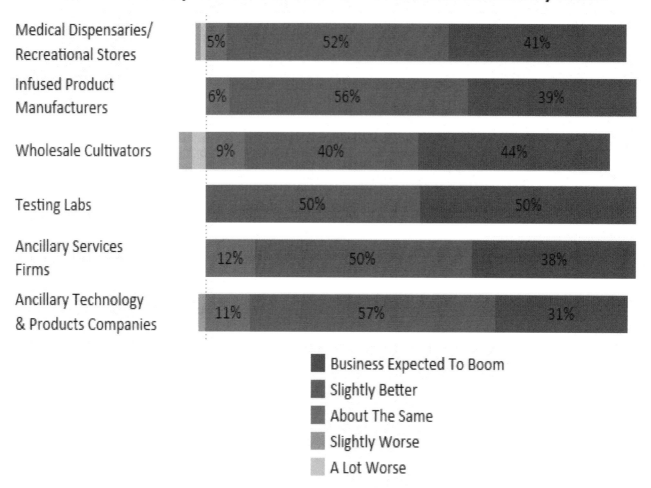

Medical Dispensaries/Recreational Stores: 5% | 52% | 41%

Infused Product Manufacturers: 6% | 56% | 39%

Wholesale Cultivators: 9% | 40% | 44%

Testing Labs: 50% | 50%

Ancillary Services Firms: 12% | 50% | 38%

Ancillary Technology & Products Companies: 11% | 57% | 31%

Legend:
- Business Expected To Boom
- Slightly Better
- About The Same
- Slightly Worse
- A Lot Worse

Source: Marijuana Business Factbook 2016

3.Cloud Technology-the process and tools that allow for transfer and storage of information. Anything that stores or allows you to pull/transmit/share information (including e-commerce) from the web is included in this category. The big boys like Apple, Microsoft, Amazon, and Google are part of this sector. The types of products in this sector include software, hardware, and online offerings, as demonstrated by the below graphic from computing.com.

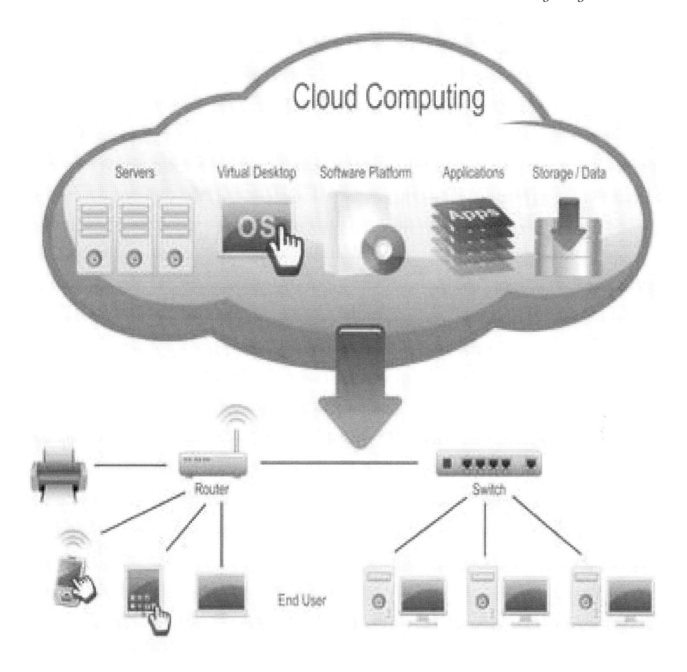

No matter what age or technological level you are at you use cloud computing, and this list will give you some idea of how far-reaching it is. The use of cloud technology is becoming the norm and is no longer an extra feature. Costly and bulky options like disc related software and storage have virtually been eliminated in favor of more efficient and less space restrictive options. Sales of cloud technology made up 85% of total IT sales in 2017 and represent a 200 billion dollar industry. Cloud computing services provide users with a series of functions including:

- Email

- Storage, backup, and data retrieval

- Creating and testing apps

- Analyzing data

- Audio and video streaming

- Delivering software on demand

Source: Azure.com

4. Artificial Intelligence (AI)-This sector revolves around products and technology that use mimicking of the human brain/personality to operate. Think Alexa, Bigsby, or Google Assistant, though there is so much more involved in this sector and new companies are emerging every day with new systems that mimic human interaction. These technologies are breaking into industries like transportation, software, e-commerce, and security. Sales and development of AI topped 108 Billion in 2018 and AI is one of the fastest growing sectors in the world. Predictions state that the following AI based industries as going to grow by at least 50% in the next 50 years:

1. Accounting-taxes and basic bookkeeping will be done by software. I mean think about it, when was the last time you went to a physical tax preparer?

2. Finance/Brokerage-most if not all investing will be done online, the onset of technology has virtually eliminated the middle person or broker.

3. Banking-online banks have exploded and teller-less banks are already becoming the norm with over 80% of deposits and transactions are done using ATMs, on Apps, or online.

4. Pharmaceuticals-using AI to tabulate the data side of research will become the norm, as well as robotic solutions in compounding elements in the lab.

5. Design-AI will soon do the majority of design tabulations for certain industries by generating precise models for blueprints and sketches.

6. Government Planning-AI will become the basis for things like smart cities and we may even become able to vote online.

7. Telecommunications-automated bill payment, payment arrangements, and even changing your plan is already becoming the norm. When was the last time you paid the

extra fee to speak with a person?

8. Purchasing-AI will soon make it possible to do automatic reordering of supplies or even to predict what is needed for a particular time span. This is already used in the restaurant industry with interactive Point of Sale, but it is being adapted for other industries as well.

9. Insurance/investments-purchasing of insurance online is already the standard, as well as making payments and making changes via many apps. In fact, new technologies allow rates to be set by tracking your actual driving behavior rather than age groups.

10. Medical Records-digital medical records have been the standard since 2005.

11. Health Care-new AI will allow surgeons to do more complex procedures by mapping down to the nano-cell and are even capable of doing some procedures on their own.

12. Transportation-self driving cars and trucks are being tested and will hit the roads within 50 years. Tesla and Uber are already testing autonomous vehicles in several cities.

See some examples below from AI.com.

Artificial Intelligence trends in 2019

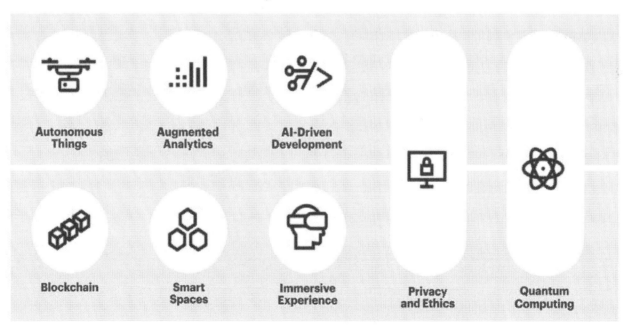

5. 5G Cellular and Wireless-5G stands for the 5th generation of wireless technology and holds

promises of speeds 100 times faster than 4G and 10 times faster than the best broadband. In the next 50 years, we will see this technology lead to autonomous vehicles, smart cities, smart factories, and much more. The download, upload, and data transfer to all devices will be seamless and further merge the global economy into a more cohesive unit. Revenue from the development and sale of 5G already tops 15.7 billion and growing. Not everyone has made the jump to 5G, but all will eventually come on board with major players like Verizon, AT&T, Sprint, China Mobile, Cisco, and Google leading the pack. The estimates are 326 billion dollars in capital will be needed to establish 5g by 2025 and to be a part of most industries by 2026. These companies will continue to experience growth and investors will be rewarded.

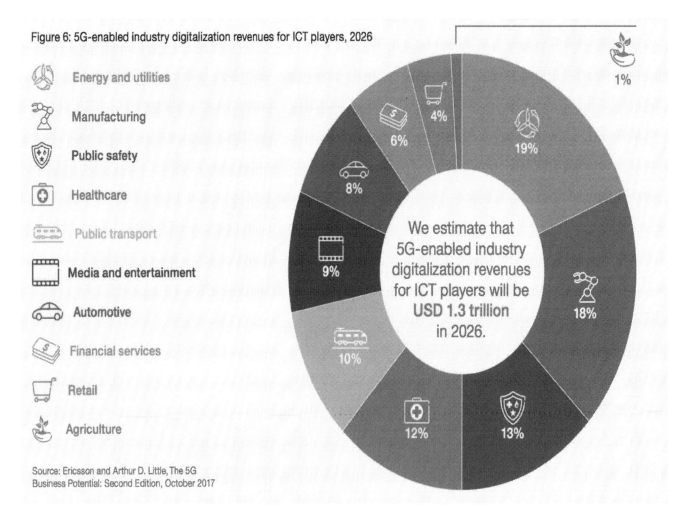

Figure 6: 5G-enabled industry digitalization revenues for ICT players, 2026

Energy and utilities

Manufacturing

Public safety

Healthcare

Public transport

Media and entertainment

Automotive

Financial services

Retail

Agriculture

We estimate that 5G-enabled industry digitalization revenues for ICT players will be USD 1.3 trillion in 2026.

Source: Ericsson and Arthur D. Little, The 5G Business Potential: Second Edition, October 2017

6. Nanotechnology-is a sector dealing with the manipulation and research of extremely small particles of 100 nanometers or less. These particles will lead to greater energy output with less strain on resources. The possibilities for the use of nano-energy in green technologies are endless and represent the hope of what will become the future technological standard as we must reduce dependence on fossil fuels and other energy sources that take up a great deal of

resources or space. Also, the ability to manipulate cellular components will propel research into genetic conditions and diseases like cancer in the future, as we can possibly cure or prevent them with the use of nanotechnology. In addition, the manipulation of microparticles of many different elements has a wide variety of consumer and personal uses as shown below.

1. **Medicine-**Nanotechnology is already being used in medicine to deliver nanoparticles that contain drugs or other substances, or that target heat or light to microorganisms and diseased cells such as cancer cells. As well as the manipulation of stem cells and other genetic material to treat and prevent disease.

2. **Electronics-**Nano electronics have already developed space saving capabilities as their weight and power consumption are significantly less than traditional electronics.

3. **Environment-**Nanotechnology has many applications aimed at improving the environment such as cleaning up polluted areas through the use of waste eating microbes or improving manufacturing methods to prevent unnecessary waste.

4. **Consumer Products-**Nanotechnology has already found its way into numerous consumer products such as skin care with micro delivery of vitamins and making fabrics flame resistant by coating fibers.

Source: cceweek.com

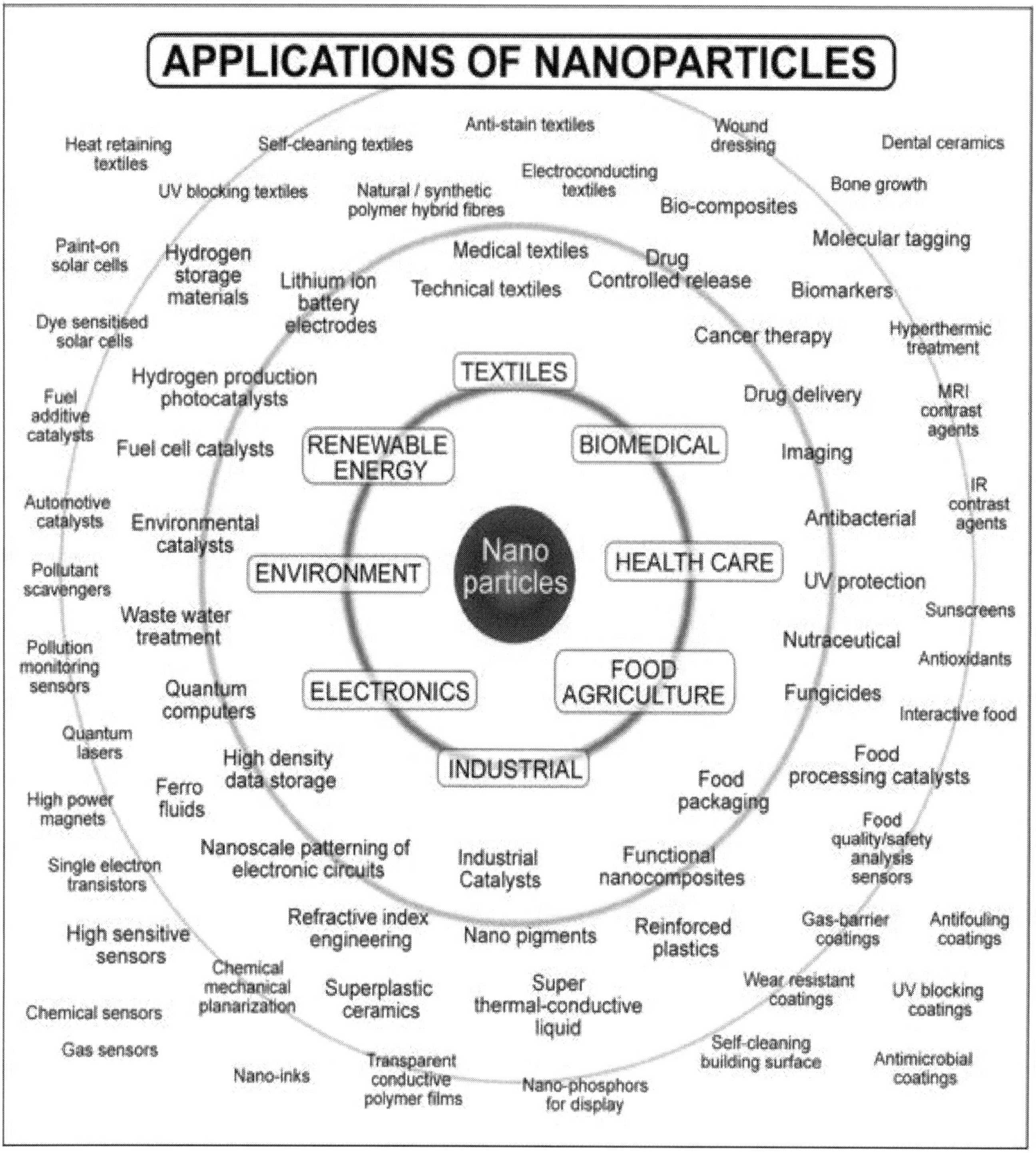
APPLICATIONS OF NANOPARTICLES
Nano particles
TEXTILES
BIOMEDICAL
HEALTH CARE
FOOD AGRICULTURE
INDUSTRIAL
ELECTRONICS
ENVIRONMENT
RENEWABLE ENERGY
Heat retaining textiles
Self-cleaning textiles
Anti-stain textiles
Wound dressing
Dental ceramics
UV blocking textiles
Natural / synthetic polymer hybrid fibres
Electroconducting textiles
Bio-composites
Bone growth
Molecular tagging
Medical textiles
Technical textiles
Drug Controlled release
Biomarkers
Cancer therapy
Hyperthermic treatment
Drug delivery
MRI contrast agents
Imaging
IR contrast agents
Antibacterial
UV protection
Sunscreens
Nutraceutical
Antioxidants
Fungicides
Interactive food
Food processing catalysts
Food packaging
Food quality/safety analysis sensors
Functional nanocomposites
Industrial Catalysts
Reinforced plastics
Gas-barrier coatings
Antifouling coatings
Wear resistant coatings
UV blocking coatings
Self-cleaning building surface
Antimicrobial coatings
Nano pigments
Super thermal-conductive liquid
Nano-phosphors for display
Superplastic ceramics
Refractive index engineering
Transparent conductive polymer films
Nano-inks
Chemical mechanical planarization
Nanoscale patterning of electronic circuits
High density data storage
Ferro fluids
Quantum computers
High sensitive sensors
Chemical sensors
Gas sensors
Single electron transistors
High power magnets
Quantum lasers
Pollution monitoring sensors
Waste water treatment
Pollutant scavengers
Environmental catalysts
Automotive catalysts
Fuel cell catalysts
Fuel additive catalysts
Hydrogen production photocatalysts
Dye sensitised solar cells
Paint-on solar cells
Hydrogen storage materials
Lithium ion battery electrodes

Chapter Two Value Stocks

How are Value Stocks Defined

Value stocks are stocks that have solid fundamentals and are priced well below their competitors in their respective fields. The determination of the "value of the stock" is based on the opinions of Wall Street Analysts, Brokers, and Peers in the same industry. As you can probably guess, this is highly speculative and not an exact science. The primary thing to remember is that value stocks are not always growth stocks. The stock is measured on its intrinsic value or true value based on factors such as its profits, P & L, stability, and potential for future growth. These are determined by many different methods and will vary by a few dollars analyst to analyst. Most of these companies will offer dividends or shares of their profits in good quarters to investors which is another source of profit and an enticement to choose the company's stock. This type of trading (with the exception of dividends) is true for not only stocks but bonds and commodities such as sugar and coffee on their own markets. These are stocks that provide income in ways other than just capital gains from sale or stock price. Though that appreciation is present, holders of value stock are more concerned with getting cash for dividends and bonuses.

Here are a few questions to ask a broker about value stocks:

- What is the status of your fund and how is it structured, do you specialize in value vs growth stocks?

- Do you have a specific industry or geographic focus for your investments and how much value is expected for value stocks?

- What are your most successful investments and what is their payout history?

- What metrics are you tracking when considering an investment in a value stock and do you keep accurate records of the payouts?

- How many investments do you make per year, and what is your typical investment size?

If you are interested, here is a list of the top value stocks of the current year

1. Eaton (ETN, $69.11) which is priced at less than 15 times trailing profits and roughly 12 times next year's projected earnings.

2. FedEx (FDX, $173.96) is still a solid business, but its growth is limited in the delivery industry.

3. Allstate (ALL, $86.49) lost almost a quarter of its value between late September and Christmas, prompted in large part by Hurricane Florence battering the East Coast and Hurricane Michael hitting the Gulf Coast.

4. AT&T (T, $30.67) is down roughly 30% from its 2016 peak, reaching fresh multi-year lows in December before bouncing back to still-depressed levels.

5. Pentair (PNR, $40.54) shares broadly continued the downward trek they began shortly before the recent spinoff was even announced.

6. Electronic Arts (EA, $90.47) is down nearly 40% of their value since their peak in 2018.

7. Caterpillar (CAT, $124.37) – Many experts say that the new tariffs and other trade regulations will cause this market price to drop, but that the dividends and other perks will make this a key value stock

8. Bank of America (BAC, $29.63) has dipped below $23 twice in the last year, but the fact that its day to day operations remain strong makes this great for income, but not growth.

9. AbbVie (ABBV, $77.14) has had a rough 2018 but overall have had some peaks and valleys that raised the price to back above $38 per share.

Value Trading vs Growth Trading

The strategy of value investing/trading was created in the 1930s by David Dodd and Ben Graham (Ivy League Finance Professors) with the publishing of their book, "Security Analysis" which has become the standard for all analysis. Until the 21st century, most traditional investing was based on value investing and relied on "reading charts" to guess what the future value of a stock would be. The intrinsic value (guessed value) minus the market price is the margin of safety and most investors would practice the risky technique of betting the stock will stay in the safety zone to make money. If you buy at the value price and then it climbs to the intrinsic price on the market then you win, if it falls below the purchase price you lose.

To protect themselves some value investors use an even more complicated hedge system of "puts" and "calls" to protect themselves in value investing. This is done on a secondary market that bundles the calls or puts them into another type of security. It consists of buying a call option on the stock or the right to buy at a low price (to protect themselves from buying high) or a put option that permits them to sell at a certain price (to protect from selling low). So, to have this type of insurance one must buy the stock, then purchase a call or put on a secondary market to "hedge" their bet on the stock. If the designated price or strike price is reached then the investor can use the hedge and someone will sell to them or buy from them at the strike price. The investor who owns the stock has the right to any gains on the stock price and any dividends, while those on the secondary market of puts and calls do not.

Wow, that all sounds complicated and it is. That is why I highly recommended the simpler method of buying growth stocks and making your profits from the rise in the price. The use of Hedge and Value Investing gave rise to the behemoth of Wall Street that you see in movies about the 1980s. This was where investment banks and brokers made their money and in many ways caused the recession of 2007. They took the model of the secondary "put and call" options and expanded it to selling things like mortgages as securities. This created a huge "middle person" giant of those that took the orders from clients and executed the trades or secondary trades.

Options may seem overwhelming, but they're actually very easy to understand if you know how to look at them. As you learn more, you may realize this is not the type of investing you are interested in, but I feel a thorough understanding of both types is needed to grow as an investor. Yes, you are starting as a simple growth investor, but as your money and expertise grow so will your interest in other types of investments. Most complex or mixed portfolios are usually constructed with several asset classes. These may be stocks, bonds, ETFs, mutual funds, preferred stocks, and alternative investments. Options are just another asset class, and when used properly, they offer many advantages to other types of investing.

They are powerful because they enhance a portfolio with added income, protection, and leverage. There is usually an option that is appropriate for any investor's goal. Often (as previously mentioned) they are used as a guard or hedge against a declining stock market or instrument to limit losses. They can also be used to produce monthly or quarterly income.

As with other types of investments, there is no guarantee with options. Trading them involves certain risks that the investor must be aware of before making a trade. In fact, you often see them sold with this or other types of disclaimers.

"Options involve risks and are not suitable for everyone. Options trading can be speculative in

nature and carry substantial risk of loss." (Source Investopedia)

Most options belong to securities known as derivatives, which are often associated with risk-taking and massive speculations. Think the speculation on home mortgages prior to 2008, they were a form of derivative. However, the overall bad perception of derivatives is really overblown. Derivative means that its price is dependent on the price of something else. Options are derivatives of other types of stocks and investments and are therefore dependent on them. On the overall standard, a stock option typically represents 100 shares of the stock.

If you buy or sell an option contract it grants you the right to buy or sell the contract but does not require you to move on the underlying asset at a set price on or before a certain date. Call options give the holder the right to buy a stock (as bundles in an option) and a put gives the holder the right to sell a stock (as bundled in the option).

To demonstrate the two types of options look at the following:

For a call option, an investor gets wind of a potential extra offering of a marijuana stock. The investor decided he or she wants the right to purchase that stock in the future, depending on certain parameters that are advantageous to the investor. These circumstances would affect their decision to buy the stock, think the USA legalizing marijuana at a future date. The investor would benefit from the option of buying or not. They can buy a call option on the stock which gives them the ability to buy the stock at $10.00 per share at any point in the next three years. They secure the purchase with a nonrefundable deposit to secure the option to call (think call for the sale).

The cost or payment is the premium for the option. It is the price of the option contract. The deposit might be $30,000 that the buyer pays for the stock. Let's say three years have passed, and the USA has legalized weed and its sub-products. The investor exercises the option and buys the stock for $10 per share, even though the price has rocketed to #20 per share. However, if legalization does not happen, the investor must still buy the stock at 10 per share, even if the price is hovering around 8 to 11 per share. That is the contract. The 30k premium is still kept as that was the price for the right to buy.

Now, as to a put option, if you own the Marijuana Stock a put option would be an insurance policy on the value of the stock in the future. The investor may fear that a bear (down) market is near and may be unwilling to lose more than 10% of their position in the stock. If the stock is currently trading at $10 per share, they can buy a put option giving the right to sell the index at

9.90 per share, at any point in the designated time period.

If the price falls to 7 in the next few years they limited their losses to 10% or pennies on the share and if the stock goes up, they are under no obligation to sell at 9.90 per share. Therefore they only lose the premium paid, unless they can later sell at a higher price.

Buying a stock instantly gives you a long position while buying a call option gives you a possible long position in the stock. If you sell a naked or uncovered call, this gives you a possible short position in the underlying stock. However, buying a put option gives you a possible short position on the stock. Selling a naked position in a put gives you a possible long position in the stock. Keeping these four possibilities straight in your head is crucial.

Finally, to understand options here are some general terms you must know.

The seller of an option is called its writer

The strike price of an option contract is the agreed price the stock in question is bought or sold.

When an option is in-the-money it means the buyer came out on the positive end of the contract.

The expiration date is the precise date that the option contract terminates.

Options can be traded on a national options exchange, such as the Chicago Board Options Exchange or CBOE, those are called listed options.

These types of options have fixed strike prices and expiration dates and each contract represents 100 shares of a stock.

The amount which an option is in-the-money is its intrinsic value.

When an option is out-of-the-money the option for the buyer is on the negative end of the purchase or sell.

The total cost or price of an option is the premium and is dependent on:

1. Stock price

2. Strike price

3. Time remaining until expiration (time value)

4. Volatility or history of the movement of the stock

Speculation is a wager or bet on the future price direction of a stock and of the derivative that the option is based on.

Hedging with options is meant to reduce risk at a reasonable cost, think of an insurance policy for stocks, this is an option.

Spreads are the difference between the strike price and purchase price.

Combinations are trades constructed with both a call and a put.

An option is the potential to participate in a future price change. So, if you own a call, you can participate in the upward movement of a stock without owning the stock. You have the option to participate or not to participate, based on your best interests.

For many of us, a middle-man is necessary in a value-based system because of the expertise required to make money. This type of expertise is something most of us do not have and we fare better in a simpler system. The secondary market has largely gone away on Wall Street with the advent of new technologies that allow the common person to trade from a computer or smartphone directly with the market, without a middle person.

Though some middle experts are needed for larger transactions, for most of us the simplicity of trading today is adequate. This new simple method is known as the Growth Market and is what we will concentrate on. Also within the realm of Value Trading is the market (Pink Sheets) that involve very small companies known as "Penny Stocks", they are companies with very cheap prices that the investor feels are poised to grow exponentially.

Bigger companies can have inflated prices since everyone's paying attention to them, while small-cap stocks tend to have fewer people that even know about them. Less risky investors stay away from them since they tend to be risky and most group investors (mutual funds) have restrictions when it comes to investing in them. They are more volatile and therefore difficult to trade.

Basics of Growth Investing

Remember you only need to be right once or twice (1000%+ returns) to secure financial freedom for the rest of your life and we will be looking at the stocks and stock strategy that can make that happen. In contrast to value investors, growth investors buy stock in companies that may be trading for more than their intrinsic or estimated value. They make decisions based on the same charts, but with the added element of market trends and past market performance. The growth investor assumes that the price or value (no matter what it is) will grow over the long term and bring them profit with the spread between the purchase price and future value. This is why people buy 500 shares of Apple or Google at 200 plus dollars a share because they see the potential for a modest profit in the future. If you choose correctly over a volume of trades that modest profit turns into a huge profit. Ultimately, growth investors seek to increase their profit through capital appreciation, much like those that flip houses or cars. The profit is in the resale price.

Growth investors seek to invest in companies whose earnings are expected to grow at a faster rate than the rest of the market average or the average of their own sectors. So they tend to focus on younger/newer companies or proven companies with growth potential. Their theory is that positive performance by the company in their actual operations will equate to better market performance and higher returns on the price of their stock. Most of these companies (as we pointed out in chapter one) are in the growth or hot industries that are developing the technologies, services, and products that will become popular or essentials in the future. The focus is entirely on growth in the stock price not on the payout of investor dividends since most of these growing companies reinvest their earnings rather than paying investors or executives.

Predicting the hot growth companies is not an exact science and it requires some case by case interpretation and judgment. No matter what method you utilize it takes a degree of both gambling instinct and hard past performance data. Investors use certain criteria as a framework for their analysis, but these methods must be applied with the company's individual situation in mind. No two companies are alike even if they operate in the same sector or develop competing products. For example, Apple and Samsung both dominate smartphone sales but are very different companies and offer products for very different types of consumers. They must each be considered on their own, apart from each other or other producers of smartphones or wireless products.

Growth stocks trade on any exchange and in any sector, but you'll usually find them in the current growth industries (which we highlighted in chapter one). However, there are some average guidelines you might use to point out yet unrecognized growth companies to invest in.

- Strong historical earnings growth. Companies should show a track record of strong earnings growth over the previous five to 10 years. The minimum EPS growth depends on the size of the company, but returns or growth that averages 3% to 10% is a good gauge. Why this range? 3% to 5% is average growth for most businesses, so choosing ones with at least that much is a good indicator of success and of course over that is just gravy. The basic idea is that if the company has displayed average to good growth in the last 5 to 10 years, it's likely to continue doing so over the next 5 to 10 years.

- Strong Earnings Reports from the company itself is a huge indicator. An earnings report is a release that outlines the company's profitability for a specific period usually for the most recently elapsed quarter or year. It's these estimates that garner a lot of attention from investors, as they are usually a great indicator of how the company will do measured against the others in the sector.

- Strong profit margins. A company's profits are calculated by deducting all expenses from sales (except taxes) and dividing by sales. It's an important metric to consider because a company can have fantastic growth in sales with poor gains in earnings. Basically, a company can show 1 billion in gross revenues, but once everything is deducted (save taxes) they may only show 10 million in earnings (taxable). This could indicate that management is not controlling costs and is allowing revenue to be eaten up by expenses. No company will survive if this ratio is off and so a company that exceeds its previous average of pretax profit margins and those of its sector could be a good growth candidate.

- Strong return on equity (ROE). This measures how much profit a company produces when compared with the money shareholders invest. It's calculated by dividing net income (revenues after taxes and expenses have been deducted) by shareholder equity (dollar amount held in shares by investors). Compare a company's present ROE to the five-year average ROE of the company and the industry. If the number is stable or increasing, then the ROE indicates that management is doing a good job protecting investor money and giving them a return on their investment (ROI).

- Strong stock performance. This is the simplest method because, in general, if a stock cannot realistically double its returns over a 10 year period than it is not a growth stock. To double in 10 years, a company's growth must be at least 7% to 10% per year for every year in the period. Some industries returns might average at a 50% growth, which only requires a 5% return year over year, so take it case by case.

Source: Bush Investments

Chapter Three Growth Portfolio Allocations

When investing, particularly for long-term goals, there are two things you will likely hear about frequently, Allocation and Diversification. Diversification helps buffer or limit an investors risk or exposure to loss in any one type of investment or one type of industry. Allocation or the range or mix of your investments will provide the guide or outline for your choices of investments. Truly understanding how the two work can help you comprise or build a portfolio that really meets your needs and goals, while only incurring your desired level of risk.

Generally, diversification deals with the process of investing in a number of different instruments to help negate risk. The basic idea is that if some of your investments in your portfolio lose or decline in value that others may increase or hold fast. For example, say you wanted to invest in mostly single or basic stocks, there is a way to diversify even in a single asset class (a type of investment). Rather than investing in just the stocks of American companies or companies based wherever you are in the world, you could mix up your portfolio or asset mix by investing in the stocks of companies in foreign nations, as well. Also, instead of just relying on "Blue Chip", large caps, or the stocks of well-known or older companies (think IBM, Google/Alphabet, Kraft Foods), you could mix it up by investing in startups or smaller/less well-known companies (small caps or medium caps).

For those of you that prefer the more stable instruments like bonds for income, you could choose a mix or both government and corporate bonds to potentially take advantage the higher returns on corporate bonds, while negating the risk with the more stable government issue bonds. Also, instead of relying on one type of maturity within bonds, you could mix it up on the maturity dates, with a mix of 5, 10, 20-year bonds, or even longer. Remember that longer-term bonds tend to react more dramatically to interest rate functions than shorter-term bonds. So, interest rates will have less effect on a five-year bond than a 20-year bond.

For those that wish to venture outside things like stocks and bonds, there is the world of currency trading on the FOREX. This is basically buying blocks of a foreign currency and then selling when its value increases. This requires a little more day trading and daily watching of the news and political events to grasp, but it is a great way to generate short term (less than 5 year) gains.

Asset allocation is a strategic way to align your portfolio with different asset classes that will maximize your returns while severely limiting your risk in a downturn. After researching all your investment goals, timeline, and fear or tolerance to risk. Then you would then invest different amounts of money (for a different percentage) of your portfolio in a range of different instruments to reach your goals while keeping your risk of loss down at a level you are willing to accept. A careful study and grasp of these three factors will guide your choices and help you make the right decisions.

Overall, a large profit margin or accumulation level, a high-risk tolerance, and a long timeline will usually translate into a more aggressive portfolio or a strategy with a higher concentration in more risky instrument types. This will naturally lead to more money or a higher percentage of your portfolio invested in long term growth investments. A common example of an aggressive or growth strategy is 70% stocks, 20% bonds, and 10% cash. On the flip side, a person whose goal is a shorter timeline, with less risk in exchange for more moderate gains would require a more conservative approach. Such a conservative or income-oriented strategy would be 50% bonds, 30% stocks and real estate, and 20% cash.

Just remember that over time, a portfolio's allocations can shift due to changing market performance. In bull (up) market years when the stock market performs particularly well, a portfolio may become heavy in stocks, while in years when bonds outperform, they may end up comprising a larger percentage of a portfolio. So, for the investor who wished to follow a formula, a little bit of rebalancing may be in order to compensate for the change in the market.

There are generally two ways to rebalance a portfolio. The first is by simply selling any over-weighted asset classes (instruments) and directing the proceeds into the under-weighted assets. The second is to direct new investments (assets) into the under-weighted asset class until the desired formula or balance is reached. Just remember to keep in mind that selling investments can result in taxes unless they are held in a tax-free or advantaged account. Think 401k sponsored retirement plan or an IRA. So, just make sure the gains from sales outweigh the taxes or a profit can quickly become a loss or a break even.

The following list shows how many times during the past 30 years each type of investment has fared positively in terms of performance. It helps show why diversification among asset classes is important.

Asset class	Number of winning years, 1987-2016
Cash	3
Bonds	5
Stocks	10
Foreign stocks	12

Source: Thomson Reuters, 2017.

Simply stated a good portfolio (your collection of investments) allocation will balance your return with your risk. Risk, what is risk? I didn't sign up for that. Unfortunately, you did, as nothing in the stock market is risk-free. Not only can you fail to profit but you can also lose the money you initially invested if you make the wrong choices. But hey that is why we are only starting with $100 for this book. You will learn the best way to allocate your investments to make sure you are profiting year after year. In the following chapter, we explore basic strategies that fit most investors.

Proper Allocation

Basic Types of Allocations

The Profit-Driven Portfolio

This portfolio focuses on making money through alternative methods like dividends or distributions to stakeholders, in addition to capital gains from the stock price. These Blue-chip or more settled companies are usually not growth stocks, but I feel compelled to mention them as you may want to add some of them as your knowledge and investment skills grow. One bright side to value stocks it that you can continue to receive dividends from them in a downturn if the company's performance is stable. The income portfolio should generate positive cash flow, bottom line. This is real cash and profits in your pocket each year. Real Estate and Bonds are usually good options for this type of portfolio, in addition to companies that return a great majority of their profits back to shareholders instead of investing all of it in growing the business. They may invest some of it into the business, but the vast majority is written off by giving it to investors for tax benefits. In this way, they pass their income through to the shareholders and pay much fewer taxes. An example of this type of company is Real Estate Investment Trusts (REITs) which pool money to flip real estate, without one person taking all the risk. Most REITs are traded on major stock exchanges, but there are also public non-listed and private REITs. The two main types of REITs are equity REITs and mortgage REITs commonly known as mREITs, but there are four major types as shown below from Reit Invester.com

Equity REITs – a company that owns or operates income-producing real estate.

Mortgage REITs – mREITs provide financing for income-producing real estate by purchasing or originating mortgages and mortgage-backed securities and earning income from the interest on these investments.

Public Non-listed REITs – PNLRs are registered with the SEC but do not trade on any major stock exchanges.

Private REITs – Private REITs are offerings that are exempt from SEC registration and whose shares do not trade on national stock exchanges.

These stocks are very tied to the economic climate, even more than most stocks, but while the real estate market is hot or rising the profits from the resales are then given back to the investors as dividends. They can take a beating when the market falls, as real estate building and buying activity dries up. So, make sure you keep abreast of this as with any non-growth stock.

This Portfolio is a nice complement to most people's salary, wage, or retirement savings. Contrary to growth investors those in this type of portfolio should look out for stocks that may have fallen out of favor but still maintain a high rate of distributions to investors. These companies not only supplement income but also provide those capital gains, as no company pays dividends if its bottom line is not healthy. In addition to REITs, bonds, utilities, and other slow-growth industries are an ideal choice for this type of portfolio.

The Aggressive Portfolio

This portfolio is as close to Reno, Vegas, or Atlantic City as you can legally get. It presents more risk than any others we will discuss. Most experts say that a maximum of 10% of one's money be used to fund this type of portfolio. Aggressive stocks can be Initial Public Offerings (IPOs) of new companies, technology or health care businesses in the process of researching a breakthrough product, or a small energy company about to release its earnings report. Aggressive Portfolios and stocks, require the most work to be traded successfully, as you do not want to buy and hold but instead to use a day trading type of strategy.

An aggressive investment strategy is generally a strategy that is designed to maximize returns by taking a relatively higher degree of risk. Strategies for achieving higher returns typically emphasize growth over time as a primary investment goal, rather than steady income or safety of your principal. This strategy would, therefore, have an investment allocation with a substantial or majority percentage in stocks or real estate and little or no investments allocated to bonds or cash.

Aggressive investment strategies are generally more suitable for young adults with smaller portfolio sizes because they usually have a lengthy investment timeline that enables them to ride out short-term market changes. They are not deterred by sudden losses early on that may have less impact than changes near the end of the timeline. Most investment advisors do not consider this strategy right for anyone else unless such a strategy is applied to only a small portion of one's total savings. Regardless of the investor's age high tolerance to risk is a prerequisite for this type of strategy. These are the key concepts of an aggressive type allocation.

- Accepts more risk in pursuit of greater return.

- Achieves its goals through one or more of many strategies including asset selection and asset allocation.

Since the 2008 recession, data shows a preference away from aggressive strategies and active management and towards passive index investing. However, for those investing aggressively, their allocation would contain the following:

Portfolio One - 75% equities and real estate, 15% fixed income, and 10% commodities.

Portfolio Two - 85% equities and real estate and 15% commodities.

Aggressive investment strategies would also utilize a higher turnover strategy, seeking to concentrate on stocks that show high return in a short time period.

Generally, an aggressive strategy needs more constant management than a conservative long-term wait and hold strategy. It is likely to be much more volatile and could require a lot of adjustments, depending on market conditions. Also, more active rebalancing would also be required to bring portfolio allocations back to their target levels. The volatility of the assets could lead mixes to deviate significantly from their original weights.

The Mixed Portfolio

A mixed portfolio means venturing into other types of investments outside of stocks. Bonds, commodities, real estate, and even art. There is a lot of flexibility in this approach and a lot of people prefer it. Traditionally, this type of portfolio would contain growth and income stocks, government or corporate bonds, and REITs. A common strategy for a hybrid portfolio would include a mix of stocks and bonds in relatively fixed proportions. This type of approach offers diversification across multiple types of investments and is more suited for a conservative type of investor.

The best way to accomplish a mixed allocation would be to look at the timeline we have for when we might need the money we're investing. Any investors that might need their money within a year's time should simply invest in an interest-bearing cash account. Period. Taking a chance and investing your cash (when you need it so soon) in bonds or stocks is not advantageous as there is a huge chance that a percentage of your money could be lost before you need it. Keeping the principal safe and liquid is the smart thing to do for any money that might be needed quickly.

Money should be invested only if it's going toward long-term goals further than five years out, such as retirement. The best investment for long-term growth is stocks because, over long periods of time, they outperform nearly all other types of investments. This is even though they may lose value in a given year.

Many financial advisors adhere to the rule of subtracting your age from 110. The answer should be the percentage of your portfolio that's invested in stocks. As a person ages, their portfolio's mix of stocks and bonds will gradually move to a more conservative mix. Investors can always tweak the formula to their own tastes if they are willing to accept more risk. A more aggressive investor may up the number to 120, allowing a 50-year-old to invest 70% of their portfolio in stocks. Many investors and advisors believe that if they increase their portfolio's range of allocation and diversify its stock and other instruments, they decrease its risk. This is not necessarily true, especially for those who spend time studying individual investments. It can be safe to allocate your funds into a diverse range within the sale asset class. For example a mix of common and preferred stock or a range of different industries.

Now that you have an understanding of what a portfolio is and how to allocate it, let's take a look at the various strategies they most investors use.

Recession Proof Stocks

Yes, they exist and we are going to take a quick look at what makes a recession-proof stock and how to recognize them. First recession is defined as an extended period of time where the elements of economic growth are sub-par such as:

1. GDP (Gross Domestic Product)-In the 2006/8 recession the GDP defined as: private consumption + gross investment + government investment + government spending + (exports – imports), dipped with losses of 2.5% and finally started creeping up in 2009.

2. Unemployment Rate (number of unemployed persons / labor force)-The unemployment rate grew to 4.9% during the 2006 to 2008 recession and has steadily decreased to a low of 3.4% currently.

3. Job Creation (number of new job creation in comparison to the previous period)-In the 2006 to 2008 recession we lost almost 3 million jobs compared to the current rate of over 300k added per quarter.

4. Income Levels (rates of wages to inflation)-The rate of wages to inflation has remained at a steady 7.25 per hour for minimum wage in most states. The rate is low and is the subject of much debate.

5. Inflation Rate (value of the dollar to the cost of goods)-We have remained at the core rate of 1.9% for many years with rates expected to climb to 2% in 2021 to 2022.

6. Strength of the Dollar (value of the dollar to other currencies)-The dollar has had a bit of roller coaster over the past 10 years, but still remains a powerful element in the world market.

With those ideas in mind, it is common sense that recession-proof stocks would be those that either assist "Main Street" with saving money or escaping the worry or stress that inevitably accompany a recession. Also, necessities like Food, Utilities, and basic transportation needs are pretty much recession proof. Here are the top recession-proof stocks that remained at least 2% (beating core inflation) growth during downturns:

- COSTCO (COST)-Current Stock Price-$243 per share, Lowest Price During Recession $189 per share

- Sam's Club and Walmart (WMT)-Current Stock Price-$102 per share, Lowest Price During Recession-$95 per share

- Walt Disney (DIS)-Current Stock Price-$133 per share, Lowest Price During Recession-$115 per share

- Netflix (NFLX)-Current Stock Price-$375 per share, Lowest Price During Recession-$325 per share

- Dollar General (DG)-Current Stock Price-$122 per share, Lowest Price During Recession-$115 per share

- Big Lots (BIG)-Current Stock Price-$37 per share, Lowest Price During Recession-$28 per share

- Spirit Airlines (SAVE)-Current Stock Price-$55 per share, Lowest Price During Recession-$50 per Share

- Molson Coors (TAP)-Current Stock Price-$60 per share, Lowest Price During Recession-$52 per share

- Constellation (marijuana) (STZ)-Current Stock Price-$205, Lowest Price During Recession (N/A)

- Canopy Growth (CGC)-Current Stock Price-$47 per share, Lowest Price During Recession (N/A)

- Cell Phone Carriers: T-Mobile (TMUS) Verizon (VZ) AT&T (T) Sprint (S) Current Stock Prices-73, 56, 31, & 5 per share, all of them held to at least 2% growth during 2006 to 2008

- Public Storage PSA S&P 500 lost 55% from 2007 - 2009; PSA shares lost 38%

- Brookfield Infrastructure Partners (BIP) S&P 500 lost 51% in 2008; BIP shares lost 43% (IPO'd in 2008)

Other stocks remained strong investments during the recession through the growth of their dividends:

- Duke Energy (DUK) S&P 500 lost 55% from 2007 - 2009; DUK shares lost 34%

  o Dividend Growth Streak: 11 years

- Digital Realty Trust (DLR) S&P 500 lost 55% from 2007 - 2009; DLR shares lost 27%

  o Dividend Growth Streak: 13 years

- WEC Energy Group (WEC) S&P 500 lost 55% from 2007 - 2009; WEC shares lost 18%

  o Dividend Growth Streak: 15 years

- Flowers Foods (FLO) S&P 500 lost 55% from 2007 - 2009; FLO shares lost 1%

  o Dividend Growth Streak: 16 years

- Magellan Midstream Partners (MMP) S&P 500 lost 55% from 2007 - 2009; MMP shares lost 30%

  o Dividend Growth Streak: 17 years

- Enterprise Products Partners (EPD) S&P 500 lost 55% from 2007 - 2009; EPD shares lost 37%

  o Dividend Growth Streak: 20 years

- Reality Income Corp (O) S&P 500 lost 55% from 2007 - 2009; O shares lost 43%

  o Dividend Growth Streak: 24 years

- Chevron (CVX) S&P 500 lost 55% from 2007 - 2009; CVX shares lost 34%

  o Dividend Growth Streak: 32 years

- Exxon Mobil Corporation (XOM) S&P 500 lost 55% from 2007 - 2009; XOM shares lost

28%

- o Dividend Growth Streak: 35 years

- Consolidated Edison (ED) S&P 500 lost 55% from 2007 - 2009; ED shares lost 26%

- o Dividend Growth Streak: 44 years

- Pepsico (PEP) S&P 500 lost 55% from 2007 - 2009; PEP shares lost 35%

- o Dividend Growth Streak: 45 years

- Kimberly-Clark (KMB) S&P 500 lost 55% from 2007 - 2009; KMB shares lost 34%

- o Dividend Growth Streak: 45 years

- Leggett & Platt (LEG) S&P 500 lost 55% from 2007 - 2009; LEG shares lost 44%

- o Dividend Growth Streak: 46 years

- Altria (MO) S&P 500 lost 55% from 2007 - 2009; MO shares lost 20%

- o Dividend Growth Streak: 49 years

- Coca-Cola (KO) S&P 500 lost 55% from 2007 - 2009; KO shares lost 31%

- o Dividend Growth Streak: 55 years

- Johnson & Johnson (JNJ) S&P 500 lost 55% from 2007 - 2009; JNJ shares lost 27%

- o Dividend Growth Streak: 56 years

- Procter & Gamble (PG) S&P 500 lost 55% from 2007 - 2009; PG shares lost 36%

- o Dividend Growth Streak: 61 years

Do you see the pattern of necessity and escape in these stocks? Keep that in mind during the next downturn with the noted characteristics of these types of stocks:

1. *The company provides critical repair/maintenance/essentials*-Consumers cut out optional services first and identify things they can do themselves instead of hiring them out. Think about household repairs, landscaping, or house cleaning.

2. *The company serves an elite or protected client*-These are both the very rich who will

continue their luxuries and those somewhat protected from the recession. Think food delivery to grocers, supplies to utility plants, and medical and pharmaceutical suppliers.

3. *The company provides products or services that are the rule of law*-They provide their services or products to people or business that run under a government mandate. Think police, fire, EMS and those that supply them, and the military.

4. *The Company provides escape or needed stress relief*-This seems trivial, but alcohol, marijuana, and home-based entertainment companies usually remain stable during times of recession. See the above list of recession-proof stocks for examples.

5. *The company provides discounted essentials or is built on bargains*-Think stores and businesses that are known for providing cheap or heavily discounted products. The list of stocks above represents discount retailers and travel providers.

Source: Investopedia

The Basic Investment Strategies

1. Value Investing

   This is the investment strategy we looked at in chapter two which is based on finding stocks that are underpriced or undervalued. The amount of chart reading and research this takes is staggering and the returns can be very slow. This a buy and hold that requires a long-term investor who is content with holding onto a stock for years to get a payoff.

2. Income or Profit Investing

   This strategy involves going heavy into Profit Stocks/Portfolios that involve companies that pay distributions and capital gains on resale price. They can provide a reliable income stream with minimal risk and because they are a long term hold and should comprise at least a small portion of every investment strategy.

3. Growth Investing

   This investment strategy focuses on capital appreciation by looking for companies that exhibit signs of above-average growth, even if the share price appears expensive in terms of metrics. This strategy is somewhat riskier and involves investing in smaller companies that have a large potential for growth in growth sectors.

4. Small Cap/Micro Cap Investing

This is for those looking to take on a little more risk in their portfolio. As the name gives away, a small-cap investor focuses on purchasing stocks from small companies who are relatively unknown and thus less expensive. Often referred to as "Penny Stocks", they are companies with very cheap prices that the investor feels are poised to grow exponentially. Bigger companies can have inflated prices since everyone's paying attention to them, while small-cap stocks tend to have fewer people that even know about them. Less risky investors stay away from them due to the risk and most group investors (mutual funds) have restrictions when it comes to investing in them. They are more volatile and therefore difficult to trade.

Whatever you decide, just remember that your goal is a balanced approach with an initial emphasis on Growth Stocks and Investing until you learn the ropes. Then you can enter into more difficult strategies. A balanced investment strategy aims to be more middle of the road and tends to meet the needs of most investors. Its goal is to balance your risk with return and seeks to create a portfolio you are comfortable with.

For example, ask yourself the following when choosing a strategy:

1. Are you wanting to preserve your capital/initial investment?

2. Do you want aggressive or fast returns?

3. Do you want steady income?

4. How long are you willing to let the money remain invested?

Even a balanced investment strategy can be rather aggressive in nature for some and is more suitable for those investors with at least five years to wait for returns. It is very appropriate for a younger investor, who has many more years to work and retirement is a distant goal. If you have a much shorter time frame in mind or a different type of goal that will occur in less than five years, a big purchase (home or vehicle) for instance, you may want to concentrate on a more conservative strategy and focus on the preservation of capital.

Preservation of capital focuses on maintaining current capital levels and preventing/limiting loss. This strategy works mainly with short term and secure investments like government bonds or Certificate of Deposits. A capital preservation strategy will work for older investors or those needing their money for a life event in less than five years. It is for those looking to maximize their current financial assets and to avoid taking significant risks with their chunk of money.

If you are young or have 10 plus years or more to play with a chunk of money you may want to consider an aggressive strategy that maximizes growth, while not concentrating too much on risk. These type of strategy would focus on a portfolio that centers on small-cap stocks, corporate bonds, junk bonds (below investment grade), FOREX (world currencies), real estate, and cryptocurrency. In general, a capital growth portfolio will contain majority stocks and bonds with a smaller amount in currency/real estate and the final bit in cash or even precious metals. Growth-oriented strategies seek high returns by definition, the mixture still protects the investor somewhat from losses on a larger scale while not concentrating too much on a small daily loss.

Why Growth Stocks to Start?

Well from the research we have done it is clear that as a new investor you want to cut your teeth on the simplest type of investment which, for someone with more than 5 years to play with, is Growth Investing. It requires the least amount of research and can yield the greatest returns over time. In fact, a simple Google Search can tell you what companies fall into this category. Simply Google:

1. Growth Industries

2. Best Stocks in the Industry

3. That company's income statements

Remember a growth stock is a share in a company that has shown faster or greater than average growth and has the potential to continue growing faster than the overall economy. The one drawback of these stocks is that because such stocks generally increase in price quicker and in a higher percentage than other stocks, they cost an average of 25% more per share than a value stock. The rapid growth is usually based on the company's current earnings and projected growth over the next 5 to 10 years. In the long run, the price you would pay for the stock is usually justified, but they also tend to be considered a riskier investment.

If a company shows stability or growth over the past 5 years, it is definitely a growth stock, but to make things easier I have compiled a detailed list of the top 100 growth stocks and how they stand at the time of publication in the next section of the book. Read on for the in-depth information.

Chapter Four Growth Stocks Part 1

Baidu (NASDAQ: BIDU)

Price at time of writing: $165.72 USD

Often dubbed the "Google of China", the Chinese search engine and online advertising leader suffered a 32% dip in 2018, but now looks like the share price has finally reached the bottom.

Chinese ad spending increased 25% year on year, and Baidu still controls roughly 70% of the online advertising space. This isn't showing any signs of slowing down either. In addition to this, the company is investing heavily in Internet of Things (IoT) technology and cloud computing, two more growth markets.

Financials are solid and third quarter sales increased by 27% on a year-on-year period.

Baidu's hidden gem is its strong relationship with the Chinese government. This is vital for any China-based stock as centralization still heavily dominates the business scene.

The big risk here is that Google makes a play to re-enter the Chinese market, which could signal the end of Baidu as the consensus number one. However, Google has tried and failed before to dominate the world's largest country.

This stock isn't for everyone, with any Chinese based stock, you must be willing to bear more volatility, but if there's a space in your portfolio for a potentially explosive growth play, Baidu is a great option.

Horizon Pharma (NASDAQ: HZNP)

Price at time of writing: $24.88 USD

Founded in 2005, this Irish Based Pharma Company in Dublin, Ireland was relocated to Chicago, IL USA. Its specialization was and remains pain and anti-inflammatory remedies.

97% of the company's sales are to US medical companies and doctors, hence the move to the states to save on shipping costs.

Current sales stand at $1.056 billion per year with the vast majority coming from outside

Ireland and the European Area.

Horizon's strengths are in its strong relationship with the USA and North American Market and its recent acquisitions of smaller Pharma companies (Raptor & Hyperion) with their patented Arthritis drugs, Procysbi and Quinsar. This gives them a substantial share in the pain management sector.

The main risks are the large amount of publicity related to the opioid crisis and the loss of patents, but as it stands it is poised for growth in the next 5 to 10 years.

This stock will remain fairly stable even in a downturn so it is appropriate for all investors.

Okta (NASDAQ: OKTA)

Price at time of writing: $99.73 USD

Founded in 1978 in the Balkan Country of Macedonia. Okta is part of the Hellenic Petroleum Group and is one of the biggest providers of fossil-based fuels and cloud software which helps companies manage and secure user authentication into modern applications in the world.

Current sales stand at $7.80 billion per year with product distribution all over the world, especially in Europe.

OTKA's strength is in its strong relationship with the Greek Government. Indeed, this company was owned by the government up until recently when they began transitioning to a private firm.

The main risk is the large amount of attention given to switching away from fossil fuel dependency and onto renewable sources of fuel. However, its other emphasis on cloud technologies will keep it solid.

This stock will remain fairly stable even in a downturn as it provides essential services and is beginning to look at green fuels production.

The fact it is linked to volatile Balkan areas may yield dips and rises more than the average investor would like, but overall it is appropriate for the long hold investor.

W.W. Grainger (NASDAQ: GWW)

Price at time of writing: $292.74 USD

Founded in 1927 in Chicago, IL this company is one of the largest suppliers of industrial supplies to factories, retailers, and construction sites. They currently have over 900 US locations and almost 100 Canadian.

Current sales stand at $10.4 billion with distribution all over the world, the majority of which remains within North America.

Its strengths are in its great reputation and history of stellar service, as well as relationships with the majority of retailers and big construction companies.

The main risks are the large stakes it has in commercial construction which slow during a downturn, but it has a healthy enough maker share with governments and retail that it has remained strong during both a depression and recession.

This stock will remain fairly stable even in a downturn as it provides essential services/products.

The fact it is linked to essential service and has a longstanding history makes it an appropriate stock for most growth investors.

West Pharmaceutical Services (NASDAQ: WST)

Price at time of writing: $115.55 USD

Founded in 1923 in Exton, PA, West Pharmaceutical Services is a designer and manufacturer of pharmaceutical packaging and delivery systems. It is one of the USA's largest producers and designers of prescription/OTC medicines and medical devices, as well as medicinal distribution and delivery of drugs.

Current sales stand at $1.7 billion per year with distribution all over the world.

Its strengths are in its strong ties to American medical companies and providers and the fact that its products are some of the most essential services. An additional strength is its great distribution chain serving Europe and the Far East, as well as North America.

It maintains average risk with the expiration of patents, but West remains a strong company for the future.

This stock will remain fairly stable even in a downturn as it provides essential services.

The fact it is linked to very stable areas will make it a good investment for most investors.

Alibaba (NASDAQ: BABA)

Price at time of writing: $187.37 USD

Founded in 1919 in the Alibaba Group at Xixi in Hangzhou, China, Alibaba is a Chinese multinational conglomerate specializing in e-commerce, retail, internet, and technology. It is one of China's largest consumer, electronics, retail, and payment providers. Think of it as the Amazon/PayPal of China.

Current sales stand at $250 Billion per year with distribution all over the world.

Its strengths are in its strong ties the Chinese Government and the fact its products make up the majority of Far East consumer products and electronic payments. Another significant strength is its great distribution chain serving the Far East

It maintains average risk despite the emerging competition in the space due to its strong sales topping Walmart, eBay, and Amazon Combined in 2015. This stock will remain fairly stable even in a downturn. Also, complaints from Western companies about substandard products will limit exposure in the West.

The fact it is linked to high sales and has a sort of monopoly in this location makes it a good fit for most investors that do not mind the volatility of the Far East.

PayPal (NASDAQ: PYPL)

Price at time of writing: $106.93 USD

Founded in 1998 in Silicon Valley, CA. It started as a subsidiary of eBay to process its payments. It became a universal payment process as an independent company in 2014.

Current sales stand at $13.9 Billion per year with users all over the world.

Its strengths are in its strong ties to the major online retailers with which it works. With online transactions making up over 70% of all transactions. In addition to online dominance, PayPal has negotiated contracts with traditional retailers and individuals for payment for service. It is a top five method of payment all over the world.

It maintains average risk with the emerging competition with retailers and individuals. PayPal continues to expand where it is taken by purchasing European payment processors like IZettle. This stock will remain fairly stable even in a downturn as money transfer is essential.

The fact it is linked to high sales and has a sort of monopoly on payment options allows it to remain strong and ideal for all investors.

Amazon (NASDAQ: AMZN)

Price at time of writing: $1927.39 USD

Founded in 1994 in Seattle, WA Amazon is a technology company that focuses on e-commerce, payment processing, cloud computing, and artificial intelligence. Amazon is the largest e-commerce marketplace and cloud computing platform in the world as measured by revenue and market capitalization. They started as a small online bookseller, but eventually expanded to become the go-to online retailer selling most consumer products and electronics. In the later 2000's it expanded into Fresh Grocery delivery by acquiring Whole Foods, AI with Alexia, and credit by partnering with several banks for credit cards, as well as expanding into Video Streaming/Production and on-demand delivery with Prime and Prime Now.

Current sales stand at $233 billion per year and climbing with users all over the world. It is by far the world's biggest retailer and shows no signs of slowing down. The main drawback is the recent allegations about employee abuse and employment violations. This seems to have been lingering for a number of years, but has died down a bit and has not caused any dip in business.

Its strengths are in its strong ties to multiple industries and its reputation as a bargain place to shop with free delivery.

It maintains average risk with the emerging competition with other retailers and tech companies. This stock will remain fairly stable even in a downturn as it sells many essentials and will be on the front lines of Finance, AI, and Cloud Computing.

The fact that it is linked to high sales and has a partial monopoly on sales allows it to remain strong and ideal for all investors.

Carvana (NASDAQ: CVNA)

Price at time of writing: $67.05 USD

Founded in 2013 in Tempe, AZ as a subsidiary of DriveTime, Carvana became independent in 2014. It started as an online car and parts retailer, but eventually expanded to become a one-stop shop for used vehicles. It is a unique experience that allows shoppers to order, customize, and finance a car for delivery or purchase from their vehicle vending machines at their physical locations.

Current sales stand at $20 million per year and climbing with online and store sales.

Its strengths are in its unique experience as an online car superstore and its vending machine option is a huge attraction if only for the novelty.

It maintains average risk with the emerging competition with other retailers and tech companies. However, this stock will remain fairly stable even in a downturn as it sells cars for rock bottom prices.

The fact that it is a low price leader will keep this a stable stock for most investors.

TriNet Group (NASDAQ: TNET)

Price at time of writing: $62.37 USD

Founded in 1988 in San Leandro, CA as a payroll provider but later expanded to become a one-stop shop for all things payroll and HR, TriNet provides important tasks for small to medium-sized companies that would normally be handled by an in-house employee for a lot less money.

Current sales stand at $3.5 billion per year and climbing as more companies outsource this type of work.

Its strengths are in its reputation and the statistics that say over 75% of companies outsource HR and payroll.

It maintains average risk with the emerging competition with other companies, but the fact it has a longstanding reputation with many established companies are in its favor.

The fact that it is an industry leader will keep this a stable stock for most investors.

Canopy Growth Corp (NASDAQ: CGC)

Price at time of writing: $47.73 USD

Canopy Growth Corp was formerly Tweed Marijuana Inc. and is a cannabis company based in

Smiths Falls, Ontario. Tweed was founded by Bruce Linton and Chuck Rifici in 2013 and renamed Canopy Growth Corporation in 2015. Since its inception in 2013, the company has remained in Ontario, Canada as one of a handful of Cannabis Companies present at the time. Canopy Growth Corp still owns over 30% of the market share.

Current sales stand at $40 million per year and climbing as the Cannabis industry expands at a rapid rate.

Its strengths are in its reputation and the fact that it was one for the first legalized producers.

It maintains average risk despite the emerging competition with other companies, especially since many countries and states still have not legalized cannabis yet. CGC remains poised as a leader as any competition will take many years to get established.

The fact it is an industry leader will keep this a stable stock for most that have no moral conflicts with investing in marijuana.

Square (NASDAQ: SQ)

Price at time of writing: $72.46 USD

Founded in 2009 in San Francisco, CA as one of less than 5 point of sale services for individuals and small businesses. Its square reader accepts credit card payments by connecting to a mobile device's audio jack. The original version consisted of a simple read head directly wired to a 3.5 mm audio jack but has expanded into having its own range of full Point of Sale units for businesses.

Current sales stand at $4.5 billion per year and climbing as the premier payment processor of small business and individual proprietors. Its strengths are in its reputation and the fact that it has become synonymous with taking payments- "we've got a square".

It maintains average risk with the emerging competition with other companies, and the fact remains that it is poised as a leader and any others have to play catch up at this point.

The fact it is an industry leader will keep this a stable stock for most investors and it has the potential to go as high as the tech sector.

Control4 (NASDAQ: CTRL)

Price at time of writing: $17.45 USD

Founded in 2003 in Draper, UT, Control4 is a leading global provider of automation, AI, surveillance, and networking for homes and businesses. It offers personalized control of lighting, music, video, comfort, security, and communications integrated into a unified smart home system that enhances the daily lives of its consumers by allowing them to control all aspects of their home from their table, computer, or smartphone. Its main product functions as a creator and designer of automation and networking systems for homes and businesses. It literally joins the multiple networks of single buildings together to allow its residents to do everything seamlessly and without extra effort or the click of a button remotely.

Current sales stand at $15.5 billion per year and climbing as the premier provider of "smart building technology". Its focus is on both on its products and infrastructure.

It maintains average risk with the emerging competition with other companies, but the fact remains that it is poised as a leader and any others have to play catch up at this point.

The fact it is an industry leader will keep this a stable stock for most investors and it has the potential to go as high as the AI sector.

Voyager Therapeutics (NASDAQ: VYGR)

Price at time of writing: $20.75 USD

Voyager Therapeutics is developing life-changing gene therapies focused on severe neurological diseases. Diseases like Parkinson's disease, Huntington's disease, Alzheimer's disease, and other neurodegenerative diseases. They were founded in 2000 by a group of neuroscientists and researchers.

Current sales stand at $12 billion per year and climbing one of the leaders in the biotech field.

Its strengths are in relationships with some of the foremost research facilities in the world.

It maintains low to average risk with the emerging competition with other companies, but the fact remains that it is still the definitive leader in the neurological area and any others have lots of research to do to catch up.

The fact it is an industry leader will keep this a stable stock for most investors and it has the potential to go as high as the tech sector.

Kinross Gold (NASDAQ: KGC)

Price at time of writing: $3.15 USD

Founded in 1993 in Toronto Ontario, Canada as one the best miners of gold and silver in North America. It currently operates eight active gold mines and was ranked fourth of the "10 Top Gold-mining Companies" of 2017 by several business publications.

Current sales stand at $3.3 million per year and climbing as one of the last full-scale extractors of precious metals. The gold and silver industries have remained stable and Kinross will continue to be one of the only players in town to do the job.

It maintains above average risk with the shrinkage of the mining industry in general, but as one of less than a handful of players, it will keep its market share. The very cheap price is one that should be bought in bulk while the price is low.

The fact it is an industry leader will keep this a stable stock for most investors and it has the potential.

Mitsubishi (NASDAQ: MSBHY)

Price at time of writing: $54.57 USD

Founded in 1871 as a manufacturer of Japanese Steamboats, no company on this list is older than Mitsubishi, it has been through several alterations and evolutions during its long history. From steamboats to insurance and then to weapons for the Japanese War effort, before it was finally revamped as a car manufacturer in the 1950s. It still remains very diverse today and is on the cutting edge of all its industries. It is the sixth-largest Japanese automaker and the nineteenth-largest worldwide by production standards. Since 2016, Mitsubishi has been almost one-third (34%) owned by Nissan and is now a part of the Renault–Nissan–Mitsubishi Alliance.

Current sales stand at $552 billion per year and climbing as its flexes it muscles across all of the following by focusing on various sectors within its industry. Some of its work includes computer/processing technology, transportation, water, electricity and industrial projects; asset management, asset financing, real estate and logistics; investment in all forms of energy including fossil fuels and renewable energy; precious metals and industrial raw ingredients; manufacturing of many types of vehicles including cars and military; and consumer products.

Its strengths are in its diversification and solid reputation across all its sectors.

It maintains low risk with the emerging competition with other companies, and the fact remains that it is hard to compete with based on size alone.

The fact it is an industry leader will keep this a stable stock for most investors and it has the potential to go as high as any of its sectors.

Vanda Pharmaceuticals (NASDAQ: VNDA)

Price at time of writing: $17.31 USD

Founded in 1999 in Germany as one of the few leaders in what are considered unmet medical needs in the areas of sleep deprivation and schizophrenia. Its drugs for these ailments are its premier products.

Current sales stand at $225 million per year and climbing as much as 17% year by year as the number one producer of mental health medicines related to mood and sleep.

It maintains low risk with the emerging competition with other companies, as few show any interest competing for its niche market share.

The fact it is an industry leader will keep this a stable stock for most investors and it has the potential to go as high as the biotech sector.

XPO Logistics (NASDAQ: XPO)

Price at time of writing: $67.05 USD

Founded in 1989 in Greenwich CE as a simple trucking company. Today XPO logistics operates in 32 countries and is the preferred logistics company for 67 of the Forbes Fortune 100 companies. It is one of the world's 10 largest providers of transportation and logistics services. XPO operates as a third-party provider in over 25 countries and has over 35,000 customers, including 70 of the Fortune 100.

Current sales stand at $17 billion per year and climbing as the premier delivery and freight company of the elites of business. It is also heavily investing in the future by working with Tesla to test the autonomous trucks and with other AI companies for Smart Distribution Centers, so it is poised for the future.

It maintains average risk with the emerging competition with other companies, but the fact remains that it is poised as a leader with deep connections to those that need their services.

The fact it is an industry leader will keep this a stable stock for most investors and it has the potential to go as high as the logistics sector.

HubSpot (NASDAQ: HUBS)

Price at time of writing: $166.23 USD

Founded in 2005 at MIT in Boston, HubSpot remains a leader in software and cloud computing solutions for social media and online advertising in general.

Current sales stand at $553 million per year and climbing as the supplier of advertising products on Facebook, Instagram, and Twitter. This is in addition to the software it provided for SEO optimization and Adwords Searches.

It maintains average risk with the emerging competition with other companies, there are very few that can turn out the number of quality products and establish the partnership with Google and Facebook that HubSpot already has.

The fact it is an industry leader will keep this a stable stock for most investors and it has the potential to go as high as the tech sector.

Veeva Systems (NASDAQ: VEEV)

Price at time of writing: $136.57 USD

Founded in 2007 in Pleasanton, CA. It is one of the few in the burgeoning industry crossover of biotech and cloud computing. It develops and services software that aids in cutting edge life science research across the globe.

Current sales stand at $100 billion per year and climbing as the premier supplier and creator of software that organizes and services the top researchers in the life, environmental, and medical fields.

It maintains low risk as emerging competition is low in the niche, and the fact remains that it is poised as a leader and any others have to play catch up at this point.

The fact it is an industry leader will keep this a stable stock for most investors and it has the potential to go as high as the tech sector.

Adobe (NASDAQ: ADBE)

Price at time of writing: $278.49 USD

Founded in 1982 in San Jose, CA as a creative software company. Adobe primarily focuses on the creation of multimedia and creativity software products, with a more recent foray towards digital marketing software.

Current sales stand at $9.3 billion per year and climbing as the premier creator and marketer of creative and not marketing software.

It maintains low risk despite the emerging competition with other companies due to the solid grip it has on the industry.

The fact it is an industry leader will keep this a stable stock for most investors and it has the potential to go as high as the tech sector.

Cerner Corp. (NASDAQ: CERN)

Price at time of writing: $63.83 USD

Founded in 1979 in Kansas City, MO as a provider of healthcare IT (HIT) software, hardware, and medical devices. Cerner Corporation is a supplier of health information technology solutions, services, devices, and hardware. Its products are in use at more than 25,000 facilities around the world. The company has more than 30,000 employees globally, with over 12,000 in its HQ in Kansas City, Missouri.

Current sales stand at $5.3 billion per year and climbing as the premier provider of HIT-related gadgets and tools to the vast majority of US and European Medical Companies.

It maintains low risk despite the emerging competition as it is generally well connected with the decision makers in the medical industry and provides stellar service and quality.

The fact it is an industry leader will keep this a stable stock for most investors and it has the potential to go as high as the bio sector.

Salesforce (NASDAQ: CRM)

Price at time of writing: $161.23 USD

Founded in 1999 in San Francisco, CA as a provider of client management and scheduling software. It has expanded to a 95% cloud-based system that primarily works with sales and service companies in the realm of client management and sales tracking. Its main product is a cloud computing service as a software (SaaS) company that specializes in customer relationship management (CRM). The software is number one for customer success and helps businesses track customer activity, sales, revenues, market to customers, and many more elements involved in customer management.

Current sales stand at $10.48 billion per year and climbing as the premier provider of sales and client tracking software and cloud-based systems. It also provides analytics, customer service, and data tracking software.

It maintains low risk despite the emerging competition in this sector as many are trying to break in this wide open niche. However, the fact remains that it is poised as a leader and any others have to play catch up at this point.

The fact it is an industry leader will keep this a stable stock for most investors and it has the potential to go as high as the tech sector.

CSX Corp. (NASDAQ: CSX)

Price at time of writing: $79.02 USD

Founded in 1980 in Jacksonville FL as a provider of rail and railroad equipment for the vast train logistics chains across the USA. Presently it has expanded into heavy equipment for industrial use and real estate holdings.

Current sales stand at $5.4 billion per year and climbing as the provider for the railroad industry and industrial real estate.

It maintains low risk with very little competition in its areas of interest and is poised for a bright future in the industry. It has invested in smart warehouse and smart car technologies that will make it the forerunner for the future of the mass transit sector.

The fact it is an industry leader will keep this a stable stock for most investors and it has the potential to go as high as the logistics sector.

Activision Blizzard (NASDAQ: ATVI)

Price at time of writing: $46.51 USD

Activision was founded in 2008 in Santa Monica, CA as a producer of film, video, and video games. Among its most popular titles are Treyarch, Infinity Ward, High Moon Studios and Toys for Bob, Call of Duty, Guitar Hero, Tony Hawk's, and Spyro/Skylanders through Activision's studios, as well as World of Warcraft, StarCraft, Diablo, Candy Crush Saga, Hearthstone, and Overwatch.

Current sales stand at $7.5 billion per year and climbing as Activision continues to release new games and update the most popular ones with new releases. In 2018, its release of Call of Duty: Black Ops 4 and its re-release of the popular game is Candy Crush Saga are just a few examples of successful new games.

It maintains average risk with the emerging competition with other companies, but the fact remains that it is the creator of some of the most popular titles in the history of gaming and it will remain a leader in the industry. The only wild card is the recently proposed regulations on the practice of microtransactions both in free games and purchased games. Within the realm of free games (like Activision's Candy Crush or Hearthstone) players are charged a few cents for advanced tactics, weapons, or tools. It is generally the only way these games make money, but the problem is that the practice has extended to paid games. This happens when you are charged money in game for more weapons/updates/designs. This resulted in many complaints and bills are being proposed to limit this. We predict no big issues, but it is something to watch.

The fact it is an industry leader will keep this a stable stock for most investors and it has the potential to go as high as the tech sector.

Expedia Group (NASDAQ: EXPE)

Price at time of writing: $125.88 USD

Founded in 1996 in Bellevue, WA as a part of Microsoft, Expedia is currently one of the largest providers of travel software and booking platforms in the world. It owns the well-known names of Hotels.com, Expedia, Travelocity, CarRentals.com, CheapTickets, HomeAway, Hotwire.com, Orbitz, Travelocity, Trivago, and Venere.com.

Current sales stand at $10.5 billion per year and climbing as the provider of the most travel booking services in the world. It has partnerships with many airlines, hotels, car rentals companies, and other leisure providers. It has the strength of exclusive cheap pricing and an excellent reputation for service.

It maintains a very low risk with the emerging competition as there is very little of it, as Expedia has the partnerships to remain the industry leader. In short, Expedia competes only with itself in this industry.

The fact it is an industry leader will keep this a stable stock for most investors and it has the potential to go as high as the tech and travel sector.

Chapter Five Growth Stocks Part 2

Emerson Electric (NASDAQ: EMR)

Price at time of writing: $73.16 USD

Founded in 1890 and currently residing in Ferguson, MO (outside St. Louis), Emerson Electric is a provider of engineering services to major manufacturers and utilities across the USA.

Current sales stand at $15.6 billion per year and climbing as the premier provider of engineering, maintenance, and support services to public utilities and manufacturers.

It maintains low risk with very little competition in the area and is poised for a bright future in the industry. Its strong relationships with many essential service providers make it strong even in a downturn.

The fact that it is an industry leader will keep this a stable stock for most investors and it has the potential to go as high as the logistics/engineering sector.

Wynn Resorts (NASDAQ: WYNN)

Price at time of writing: $143.44 USD

Founded in 2002 and currently residing in Los Vegas, NV, Wynn Resorts is a provider of gambling, entertainment, and leisure across many properties in the Western and Eastern portions of the USA. One of its major properties opened during the 2006 recession and maintained decent profits, so they are in it for the long haul.

Current sales stand at $4.4 billion per year and climbing as the premier provider of leisure services.

It maintains low risk due to the strong ties to state gaming commissions and Native American Tribes that manage many of its properties. Its strong relationship with the aforementioned entities allows it to remain strong even in a downturn.

The fact it is an industry leader will keep this a stable stock for most investors and it has the potential to go as high as the gaming sector.

Crocs (NASDAQ: CROX)

Price at time of writing: $26.85 USD

Founded in 2002 and currently residing in Boulder, CO, Crocs is a provider of footwear and apparel for men, women, and children. Originally founded to make light foam shoes for boaters and fishermen.

Current sales stand at $1 billion per year and climbing as the brand has caught on with the general public and has found their way into the pop culture.

It maintains low risk with very little competition within its niche and is poised for a bright future in the industry. Its strong relationships with many huge retailers and brand loyalty from its wearers confer strength to its position in the market.

The fact it is an industry leader will keep this a stable stock for most investors and it has the potential to go as high as the clothing sector.

Twilio (NASDAQ: TWLO)

Price at time of writing: $130.23 USD

Founded in 2008 and currently residing in San Francisco, CA, Twilio is a provider of web-based communication to businesses and allows the use of its APIs to complete a variety of communications like texts/calls via their databases. It is very comparable to Slack and Skype and has excelled in partnering with other top companies such as LuLulemon. Twilio supports the development of open-source software and regularly makes contributions to the open-source community. They recently launched OpenVBX, an open-source product that lets business users configure phone numbers to receive and route phone calls. It also sponsors Localtunnel which enables software developers to expose their local development environment to the public internet. The fact that it supports open source makes it a darling of the tech world.

Current sales stand at $650 million per year and climbing as the premier provider of these services to major companies and government entities.

It maintains low risk with very little competition in the area and is poised for a bright future in

the industry. Its strong relationships with many large companies and its cutting edge research to improve its communication system are key to keeping it strong.

The fact it is an industry leader will keep this a stable stock for most investors and it has the potential to go as high as the tech sector.

LuLulemon (NASDAQ: LULU)

Price at time of writing: $176.17 USD

Founded in 1998 and currently residing in Vancouver BC, Canada, Lululemon is a provider of athletic apparel for women and men. It has evolved from an athletic brand into a designer brand known for comfort, style, and quality.

Current sales stand at $2.6 billion per year and climbing as it has become a high fashion brand with a thriving resale market online.

It maintains low risk with very little competition as its resellers and those that wear it are fiercely loyal. In addition, the fact that a garment can last years, even under high use makes it a good fit for those looking to get the most for their money.

The fact it is an industry leader will keep this a stable stock for most investors and it has the potential to go as high as the designer/athletic clothing sectors.

MongoDB (NASDAQ: MDB)

Price at time of writing: $136.97 USD

Founded in 2007 and currently residing in NY, NY, MongoDB is a provider of database management services in a cloud environment to millions of users. It allows businesses to manage their own database of information, without having to maintain servers and other bulky items.

Current sales stand at $25 billion per year and climbing as the premier provider of data management for a host of retailers, companies, and small businesses.

It maintains low risk with very little competition in the area and is poised for a bright future in

the industry. Its strong relationships with many businesses and stellar track record for service and research will keep it strong.

The fact it is an industry leader will keep this a stable stock for most investors and it has the potential to go as high as the logistics/engineering sector.

Sarepta Therapeutics (NASDAQ: SRPT)

Price at time of writing: $116.86 USD

Founded in 1980 in Cambridge, MA, Sarepta Therapeutics is a provider of research and pharmaceuticals geared toward anti-viral treatments and respiratory ailments. Some of its major products are known for treating West Nile Virus, Hepatitis, and Pneumonia.

Current sales stand at $5.5 billion per year and climbing as the premier provider of these drugs to hospitals, clinics, and medical professionals.

It maintains low risk with he very little competition in the area and is poised for a bright future in the industry. Its strong reputation with respiratory and viral research will make it a leader for many years.

The fact it is an industry leader will keep this a stable stock for most investors and it has the potential to go as high as the biotech sector.

Netflix (NASDAQ: NFLX)

Price at time of writing: $377.23 USD

Founded in 1997 in Los Gatos, CA, Netflix began with mail-order DVD rentals and has since morphed into the leader in digital streaming and a provider of original movies and programming.

Current sales stand at $15.7 billion per year and climbing as the premier provider of these services worldwide. Recently released financial statements show consistent growth from month to month, indicating that its business model is effective.

It maintains low risk with very little competition in the niche of the one-stop streaming shop and an independent studio. The only other platforms close are HULU and AMAZON, but the former's ties to cable TV and the latter's emphasis on retail rather than streaming makes Netflix the clear winner. Netflix is poised for a bright future in the industry. Its strong relationship with many large companies and its cutting edge research to improve its communication system are key to keeping it strong.

The fact it is an industry leader will keep this a stable stock for most investors and it has the potential to go as high as the tech sector.

Qualcomm (NASDAQ: QCOM)

Price at time of writing: $88.10 USD

Founded in 1985 in San Diego, CA, Qualcomm is a provider of semiconductor and wireless communications equipment worldwide. They provide the guts that make the wireless data market work such as towers, antennas, and fiber optics.

Current sales stand at $22.7 billion per year and climbing as the premier provider of these services to major companies and government entities.

It maintains low risk with very little competition in the area and is poised for a bright future in the industry. Its strong relationship with many large companies and its cutting edge research to improve its systems and keep up with every generation of wireless data are fundamental to its strong position in the industry.

The fact it is an industry leader will keep this a stable stock for most investors and it has the potential to go as high as the tech sector.

Alphabet Inc. (NASDAQ: GOOGLE)

Price at time of writing: $12733.88 USD

Founded in 2015 and currently residing in Mountain View, CA, Alphabet Inc. is the parent company of Google which is the number one search engine in the world. In addition, they own YouTube the 2nd largest search engine, as well as being the go-to company for advertising, research, and AI.

Current sales stand at $136 billion per year and climbing as the premier provider of these services to major companies, individuals, and government entities.

It maintains low risk with very little competition in the area and is poised for a bright future in the industry. Its strong relationship with many large companies and its cutting edge research to improve its market reach is key to keeping it strong.

The fact it is an industry leader will keep this a stable stock for most investors and it has the potential to go as high as the tech sector.

iRobot (NASDAQ: IRBT)

Price at time of writing: $103.36 USD

Founded in 1990 by 3 MIT students in Cambridge, MA and currently residing in Bedford, MA, iRobot is a provider of AI-based home products like the Roomba. It is also developing a line of police, fire protection, and military robots. It has an exclusive agreement with the military for battle robots and is the largest provider of personal robots in the world, the most commonly known of which is the Roomba.

Current sales stand at $1.79 billion per year and climbing as the premier provider of these products to the military and individuals.

It maintains low risk with very little competition in the area of homes based AI gadgets and is poised for a bright future in the industry. Its strong relationship with many large retailers and its cutting edge research to improve its products and expand its offerings into the new sector of smart homes will keep iRobot a strong player in the industry.

The fact it is an industry leader will keep this a stable stock for most investors and it has the potential to go as high as the tech and AI sector.

Facebook (NASDAQ: FB)

Price at time of writing: $183.20 USD

Founded in 2004 in Cambridge MA by four Harvard Students and currently residing in Silicon

Valley, CA, Facebook provides the largest social media platform in the world with 40 billion active users. It also provides one of the largest advertising and marketing platforms in the world between FB and its acquisition of Instagram.

Current sales stand at $56 billion per year and climbing as the premier provider of these services to major companies, individuals and government entities. Its recently released balance sheets show consistent growth, indicating that it has a strong business model.

It maintains low risk with very little competition in the area and is poised for a bright future in the industry. Its strong relationship with many large companies and its cutting edge research to improve its platform is key to keeping it strong.

The fact it is an industry leader will keep this a stable stock for most investors and it has the potential to go as high as the tech sector.

JD.com (NASDAQ: JD)

Price at time of writing: $29.50 USD

Founded in 1998 and currently residing in Beijing China, JD.com is a provider of e-commerce and consumer products in China and the Far East.

Current sales stand at $65 billion per year and climbing as the premier provider of these services to the areas around China.

It maintains low risk with very little competition in the area and is poised for a bright future in the industry. Its strong relationships with many local governments and its cutting edge research to improve its operations are key to keeping it strong.

The fact it is an industry leader will keep this a stable stock for some investors (that are not bothered by the volatility of China) and it has the potential to go as high as the tech sector.

Shake Shack (NASDAQ: SHAK)

Price at time of writing: $61.25 USD

Founded in 2004 and currently residing in New York, NY, Shake Shack is a provider of fast-casual food and shakes in a clean and inexpensive environment. It started as a simple hot dog cart and has grown to a chain with 200 locations in both the US and foreign countries.

Current sales stand at $650 million per year and climbing as a premier provider of American style food in a quick clean environment. They are a few steps above typical fast food and have better service and ingredients. Think Chipotle for American style food.

It maintains low risk with very little competition in the area of fast casual burgers/shakes and is poised for a bright future in the industry. Its strong reputation and fast expansion within the niche system is key to keeping it strong.

The fact it is an industry leader will keep this a stable stock for most investors and it has the potential to go as high as the food sector.

Tesla (NASDAQ: TSLA)

Price at time of writing: $263.33 USD

Founded in 2003 and currently residing in Palo Alto, CA, Tesla is the premier provider of renewable energy and electric cars to the USA and the world. In fact, they have done so well that when one thinks of an electric car, they think Tesla.

Current sales stand at $21.4 billion per year and climbing as the premier provider of these services to major companies, individuals, and government entities.

It maintains low risk with very little competition in the area and is poised for a bright future in the industry. Its strong relationship with many large companies and its cutting edge research to improve its products is key to keeping it strong.

The fact it is an industry leader will keep this a stable stock for most investors and it has the potential to go as high as the tech sector.

Nike (NASDAQ: NKE)

Price at time of writing: $88.50 USD

Founded in 1964 and currently residing in Beaverton, OR, Nike is a provider of athletic equipment, apparel, and shoes for individuals, teams, and companies. One of the largest in the niche with exclusive contracts with many of the professional, high school, and college sports teams and leagues. Its revenues continue to climb year after year as evident in their recently released financial statements, which can be found on their website.

Current sales stand at $36 billion per year and climbing as the premier provider of these services and products.

It maintains low risk with very little competition in the area and is poised for a bright future in the industry. Its strong relationship with many large companies, sports leagues, and colleges and its cutting edge research to improve products will keep it strong.

The fact it is an industry leader will keep this a stable stock for most investors and it has the potential to go as high as the sports sector.

Boeing (NASDAQ: BA)

Price at time of writing: $376.76 USD

Founded in 1916 in Seattle, WA and currently residing in Chicago, IL, Boeing is a provider of aircraft, weapons, and military equipment for the US government, Allies, and airlines. In addition to providing the Boeing Jet Series, it also has exclusive duties with many government entities for year 2018/2019.

Current sales stand at $102 billion per year and climbing as the premier provider of these services to major companies and government entities. It has contracts with both the USA and its Allies for military equipment.

It maintains low risk with very little competition in the area and is poised for a bright future in the industry. Its strong relationships with the government and large companies and its cutting edge research to improve its products are key to keeping it strong.

The fact that it is an industry leader will keep this a stable stock for most investors and it has the potential to go as high as the tech sector.

Visa (NASDAQ: V)

Price at time of writing: $161.68 USD

Founded in 1958 and currently residing in Foster City, CA, Visa is the number one provider of branded credit, debit, and prepaid charge cards in the world. In addition, it provides payment processing and financial support to many banks and financial institutions.

Current sales stand at $18 billion per year and climbing as the premier provider of these services to major banks, companies, and government entities.

It maintains low risk with very little competition in the area and is poised for a bright future in the industry. Its strong relationship with many large companies and its cutting edge research to improve its communication system is key to keeping it strong.

The fact it is an industry leader will keep this a stable stock for most investors and it has the potential to go as high as the tech and finance sector.

Nokia (NASDAQ: NOK)

Price at time of writing: $5.83 USD

Founded in 1865 and near Helsinki, Finland as a pulp mill, Nokia is currently a provider of web-based communication, wireless communication devices, smart devices, and sell their support system to businesses, schools, and individuals.

Current sales stand at $22.5 billion per year and climbing as one of the premier providers of these services to major companies, individuals, and government entities.

It maintains average risk despite the competition in the area and is poised for a bright future in the industry. Its strong relationship with many large companies and its cutting edge research to improve its communication system is key to keeping it strong.

The fact it is an industry leader will keep this a stable stock for most investors and it has the potential to go as high as the tech sector.

Skyworks Solutions (NASDAQ: SWKS)

Price at time of writing: $89.73 USD

Founded in 2002 and currently residing in Woburn, MA, Skyworks Solutions is a provider of semiconductors, sound adapters, and wireless networking systems for wireless infrastructure.

Current sales stand at $3.2 million per year and climbing as a rising provider of these services to major companies and government entities.

It maintains average risk with the limited competition in the area and is poised for a bright future in the industry. Its strong relationship with many large companies and its cutting edge research to improve its communication system is key to keeping it strong.

The fact it is an industry leader will keep this a stable stock for most investors and it has the potential to go as high as the tech sector.

Samsung (NASDAQ: SSNLF)

Price at time of writing: $44.20 USD

Founded in 1937 and currently residing in Seoul, South Korea, Samsung is a provider of wireless communication devices, smart technology, and is a leader in the research around it.

Current sales stand at $210 billion per year and climbing as the premier provider of these services to major companies and government entities. It stands as the number one provider of wireless equipment, even taking a leading position above Apple.

It maintains low risk even with some prime competition in the sector and is poised for a bright future in the industry. Its strong relationship with many large companies and its cutting edge research to improve its communication system is key to keeping it strong. Also, Samsung has become the go-to company for manufacturers using android based systems and products and will continue to grow within that niche.

The fact it is an industry leader will keep this a stable stock for most investors and it has the potential to go as high as the tech sector.

United Technologies (NASDAQ: UTX)

Price at time of writing: $139.14 USD

Founded in 1934 and currently residing in Farmington, CE, United Technologies is a provider of engines, HVAC components, security systems, elevators/escalators, and other industrial products. It has many subsidiaries, a few of them are shown below as listed on their website.

- Otis Elevator Company: Manufacturer, installer, and servicer of elevators, escalators, and moving walkways.

- Pratt & Whitney: Designs and builds aircraft engines and gas turbines.

- Collins Aerospace: Designs and manufactures aerospace systems for commercial, regional, corporate and military aircraft.

- UTC Climate, Controls & Security: Makes fire detection and suppression systems, access control systems. Conditioning, and refrigeration systems.

- United Technologies Research Center (UTRC): A centralized research facility.

Current sales stand at $66 billion per year and climbing as the premier provider of these services to major companies and government entities. Earnings reports show strong growth, indicating that it is a major player with a successful business model.

It maintains low risk with very little competition in the area and is poised for a bright future in the industry. Its strong relationship with many large companies and its cutting edge research to improve its communication system is key to keeping it strong.

The fact it is an industry leader will keep this a stable stock for most investors and it has the potential to go as high as the logistics sector.

Clorox (NASDAQ: CLX)

Price at time of writing: $153.39 USD

Founded in 1916 and currently residing in Oakland, CA, Clorox is a provider of both chemicals, consumer products, and food products for consumers. It operates under several well-known brands like Burt's Bees and many others.

Current sales stand at $6.1 billion per year and climbing as the premier provider of these products to consumers.

It maintains low risk with very little competition in the area and is poised for a bright future in

the industry. Its strong relationships with many large companies and consumer brand loyalty indicate that it will remain a strong player.

The fact it is an industry leader will keep this a stable stock for most investors and it has the potential to go as high as the retail sector.

Duke Energy (NASDAQ: DUK)

Price at time of writing: $89.42 USD

Founded in 1904 and currently residing in Charlotte, NC, Duke Energy is a provider of energy and utilities to many customers across the USA, Canada, and South America. Duke Energy now has many subsidiaries, both in the USA and internationally.

Current sales stand at $22 billion per year and climbing as the premier provider of these services to major utilities and government entities. It operates 10% of the major utilities in the USA.

It maintains low risk with very little competition in the area and is poised for a bright future in the industry. Its strong relationship with many large companies is key to keeping it strong.

The fact it is an industry leader will keep this a stable stock for most investors and it has the potential to go as high as the biotech and utilities sectors.

Chapter Six Growth Stocks Part 3

Realty Income (NASDAQ: O)

Price at time of writing: $69.96 USD

Founded in 1950 and currently residing in San Diego, CA, Realty Income was originally a real estate management company but now is a REIT. This, as you remember from earlier chapters, pools money for investment in real estate and pays dividends based on the profits. This is a rare thing as it is both growth and income stock.

Current sales stand at $1.25 billion per year and climbing as the premier provider of investment in commercial and industrial properties.

It maintains low risk with very little competition in the area and is poised for a bright future in the industry. Its strong relationship with many large companies and the ability to buy larger properties will keep it ahead of the game.

The fact it is an industry leader will keep this a stable stock for most investors and it has the potential to go as high as the real estate sector. Even in a downturn, it will remain stable.

3M (NASDAQ: MMM)

Price at time of writing: $218.52 USD

Founded in 1902 and currently residing in Maplewood, MN, 3M was originally a mining company but now has a huge stake in the consumer product manufacturing, healthcare, security, and marketing sectors.

Current sales stand at $31 billion per year and climbing as the premier provider of these services to individuals. They also have a significant degree of brand loyalty in their manufactured brands. With a strong recent income report published to their website, 3M is set to remain successful.

It maintains low risk with its diversified businesses. Its strong relationship with many large companies and its consumer brand loyalty and reputation will keep it strong.

The fact it is an industry leader will keep this a stable stock for most investors and it has the potential to go as high as the many sectors it works in.

Starbucks (NASDAQ: SBUX)

Price at time of writing: $75.35 USD

Founded in 1971 and currently residing in Seattle, WA, Starbucks is a provider of coffee and cafe items across thousands of locations nationwide and internationally.

Current sales stand at $23 billion per year and climbing as the premier provider of these products to the public through 20,000 stores in 62 countries around the world, and growing.

It maintains low risk even with the competition in the area and is poised for a bright future in the industry. Its strong relationship with many large companies and its cutting edge research to improve its communication system are key to keeping it strong.

The fact it is an industry leader will keep this a stable stock for most investors.

Abbvie (NASDAQ: ABBV)

Price at time of writing: $78.63 USD

Founded in 2013 and currently residing in near Chicago, IL, Abbvie is a provider of cancer drugs and research and is a spinoff of Abbott Labs.

Current sales stand at $32 billion per year and climbing as the premier provider of these drugs.

It maintains low risk with very little competition in the area and is poised for a bright future in the industry. Its strong relationship with many large companies and its cutting edge research to improve current drugs develop new ones is a boon.

The fact it is an industry leader will keep this a stable stock for most investors.

TD Bank (NASDAQ: TD)

Price at time of writing: $55.61 USD

Founded in 1965 and currently residing in Toronto, Canada, TD Bank is Canada's largest bank and financial institution.

Current sales stand at $36 billion per year and climbing as the premier provider of these services to major companies and government entities.

It maintains low risk with very little competition in the area and is poised for a bright future in the industry. Its strong relationship with many large companies and its cutting edge research to improve its communication system is key to keeping it strong.

The fact it is an industry leader will keep this a stable stock for most investors.

Altria (NASDAQ: MO)

Price at time of writing: $54.58 USD

Founded in 1985 and currently residing in Henrico County, VA, Altria is a rebranding of the tobacco company Philip Morris.

Current sales stand at $27 billion per year and climbing as the company revamps to stop the damage of the no-smoking campaign. It is venturing into the e-cig market and exploring areas such as cannabis.

It maintains average risk with very little competition in the area and but is the riskiest of the growth stocks as it must overcome its past. Its strong relationship with many large companies and its cutting edge research to improve and expand its offerings will keep it stable in the future.

The fact it is an industry leader will keep this a stable stock for most investors but due to past industry shifts, it should be watched closely.

International Paper (NASDAQ: IP)

Price at time of writing: $44.63 USD

Founded in 1898 in New York by a merging of 17 paper mills and currently residing in Memphis, TN, International Paper is a provider of paper and paper products to the US government and other governments as well as private companies.

Current sales stand at $21 billion per year and climbing as the premier provider of these services to major companies and government entities. It restructured in 2006 to become much leaner and offset the paperless revolution. It is researching other potentially useful materials like hemp and other alternatives to paper.

It maintains low risk with very little competition in the area and is poised for a bright future in the industry. Its strong relationship with many large companies and its cutting edge research to improve and diversify its products is a pro.

The fact it is an industry leader will keep this a stable stock for most investors. However, it is in a shrinking industry so keep your eye on this one.

Cisco (NASDAQ: CSCO)

Price at time of writing: $56.85 USD

Founded in 1985 and currently residing in San Francisco, CA, Cisco is a provider of web-based services and hardware/software, as well as infrastructure components to enable the use of Wi-Fi and net technologies.

Current sales stand at $46 billion per year and climbing as the premier provider of these services to major companies and government entities. Its growth is demonstrated by its past year's income available on their website.

It maintains low risk with very little competition in the area and is poised for a bright future in the industry. Its strong relationship with many large companies and its cutting edge research to improve its communication system are key to keeping it strong.

The fact it is an industry leader will keep this a stable stock for most investors.

CVS (NASDAQ: CVS)

Price at time of writing: $52.96 USD

Founded in 1996 and currently residing in Woonsocket, RI, CVS is a provider of medical research and pharmacy services to businesses, medical professionals, and individuals

Current sales stand at $184 billion per year and climbing as the premier provider of these services to major companies and the general public. It has consistently grown and has expanded into health clinics and insurance.

It maintains low risk with limited competition in the area and is poised for a bright future in the industry. Its strong relationship with many large companies and its cutting edge research to improve its offerings is key to keeping it strong.

The fact it is an industry leader will keep this a stable stock for most investors.

Walgreens (NASDAQ: WBA)

Price at time of writing: $53.52 USD

Founded in 1901 and currently residing in Chicago, IL, Walgreens is a provider of medical research and pharmacy services to businesses, medical professionals, and individuals

Current sales stand at $183 billion per year and climbing as the premier provider of these services to major companies and government entities as well as the general public.

It maintains low risk with limited competition in the area and is poised for a bright future in the industry. Its strong relationship with many large companies and its cutting edge research to improve its offerings are key to keeping it strong.

The fact it is an industry leader will keep this a stable stock for most investors.

Molson Coors (NASDAQ: TAP)

Price at time of writing: $63.87 USD

Founded in 2005 via a merger between Molson of Canada and Coors Co. and currently residing in Denver, CO, it is a major provider of beer and other alcoholic beverages/consumer products worldwide.

Current sales stand at $4.8 billion per year and climbing as the premier provider of these services to major companies and government entities.

It maintains average risk despite the competition in the sector and is poised for a bright future in the industry. Its strong relationship with many large wholesalers and its cutting brand loyalty and reputation for value will keep it strong.

The fact it is an industry leader will keep this a stable stock for most investors and since beer is usually stable during downturns you don't need to fear a recession.

NXP Semiconductors (NASDAQ: NXPI)

Price at time of writing: $100.49 USD

Founded in 1953 and currently residing in the Netherlands, NXP Semiconductors is a provider of semiconductors and infrastructure components for the wireless industry.

Current sales stand at $9 billion per year and climbing as a premier provider of these services to major companies and government entities around the world.

It maintains low risk with very little competition in the area and is poised for a bright future in the industry. Its strong relationships with many large companies and its cutting edge research to improve its communication system are key to keeping it strong. In addition, it has one of the best supply and distribution chains in the world including China, Thailand, Japan, Europe, and the USA.

The fact it is an industry leader will keep this a stable stock for most investors.

Viacom (NASDAQ: VIA)

Price at time of writing: $36.66 USD

Founded in 2013 and currently residing in NY, NY, Viacom is a worldwide entertainment provider. It was formed by a merger and consolidation between CBS and other media companies.

Current sales stand at $12.5 billion per year and climbing as the premier provider of these services to the world. Its holdings have a foothold in TV and movies and include well-known names such as Paramount and Nickelodeon.

It maintains average risk despite the competition in the area and is poised for a bright future in the industry. Its strong relationship with many large companies and its cutting edge research to improve its communication system are key to keeping it strong.

The fact it is an industry leader will keep this a stable stock for most investors.

Kraft Heinz (NASDAQ: KHC)

Price at time of writing: $32.70 USD

Founded in 2015 and currently residing in Pittsburg, PA and Chicago, IL, the company is a merger of the companies Kraft and Heinz. It is a provider of consumer products and foods.

Current sales stand at $6.5 billion per year and climbing as the premier provider of these products with unrivaled brand loyalty. Its recently published sales chart can be accessed from its website and shows consistent growth each year.

It maintains low risk with very little competition in the area and is poised for a bright future in the industry. Its strong relationship with many large companies and its ever-expanding brand list keeps it an industry leader.

The fact it is an industry leader will keep this a stable stock for most investors.

Tencent (NASDAQ: TCTZF)

Price at time of writing: $49.76 USD

Founded in 1998 and currently residing in China, Tencent is a conglomerate that produces a wide range of technology including AI, wireless products, telecommunications, and consumer products. Some of its well-known products are video games, online payments (Paipal), e-commerce, and the search engine Soso. In addition, they are a Google AdSense partner and run their own social media platform known as TencentQ.

Current sales stand at $300 billion per year and climbing as the premier provider of these services to major companies and Far East government entities.

It maintains low risk with very little competition in the area and is poised for a bright future in the industry. Its strong relationship with many large companies and its cutting edge research to improve its communication system are key to keeping it strong.

Huya (NASDAQ: HUYA)

Price at time of writing: $22.72 USD

Founded in 2008 and currently residing in San Francisco, CA, Huya is a provider of web-based communication to businesses and allows the use of its APIs to perform a variety of communications like texts/calls via their databases.

Current sales stand at $650 million per year and climbing as the premier provider of these services to major companies and government entities.

It maintains low risk with very little competition in the area and is poised for a bright future in the industry. Its strong relationship with many large companies and its cutting edge research to improve its communication system are key to keeping it strong.

Weibo (NASDAQ: WB)

Price at time of writing: $70.40 USD

Founded in 2008 and currently residing in San Francisco, CA, Weibo is a provider of web-based communication to businesses and allows the use of its APIs to enable a variety of communications like texts/calls via their databases.

Current sales stand at $650 million per year and climbing as the premier provider of these services to major companies and government entities.

It maintains low risk with very little competition in the area and is poised for a bright future in the industry. Its strong relationship with many large companies and its cutting edge research to improve its communication system are key to keeping it strong.

It is a good investment for anyone not scared of investment in China.

China Mobile (NASDAQ: CHL)

Price at time of writing: $47.14 USD

Founded in 1997 and currently residing in Hong Kong, China Mobile is a provider of wireless communications and wireless products. It is semi owned by the Chinese Government and enjoys a great deal of protections that others do not have.

Current sales stand at $16 billion per year and climbing as the premier provider of these services to major companies and government entities.

It maintains low risk with very little competition in the area and with the protection of the Chinese government, it is quickly expanding into rural areas of the country with unprecedented ability to cut consumer costs. Its strong relationship with many large companies and its cutting edge research to improve its communication system are key to keeping it strong.

It is a good investment for those not worried about potential fluctuations in the Chinese market.

Aurora Cannabis (NASDAQ: ACB)

Price at time of writing: $9.14 USD

Founded in 2013 and currently residing in Edmonton AB, Canada, Aurora Cannabis is a provider of marijuana and related products.

Current sales stand at $18 million per year and climbing as a premier provider of these services to all areas where marijuana is legal (and probably some that are not).

It maintains low risk with very little competition in the area and is poised for a bright future in the industry.

It is a good investment for anyone not scared of investment in cannabis or foreign businesses.

Aphria (NASDAQ: APHA)

Price at time of writing: $7.87 USD

Founded in 2014 and currently residing in Toronto, Canada, Aphria is a provider of marijuana and related products, mostly to the medical industry.

Current sales stand at $36 million per year and climbing as a premier provider of these services to all areas in the medical arena, which provides a much bigger market than some of its competitors that rely on the recreational market alone.

It maintains low risk with very little competition in the area and is poised for a bright future in the industry.

It is a good investment for anyone not scared of investment in cannabis or foreign businesses.

Tilray (NASDAQ: TLRY)

Price at time of writing: $51.24 USD

Founded in 2014 and currently residing in Narimo BC, Canada, Tilray is a provider of marijuana and related products.

Current sales stand at $30 million per year and climbing as a premier provider of these services, with distribution and branches in Germany, South America, Australia, and New Zealand. This provides a much bigger market than some of its competitors that rely on the North American market.

It maintains low risk with very little competition in the area and is poised for a bright future in the industry.

It is a good investment for anyone not scared of investment in cannabis or foreign businesses.

Intel (NASDAQ: INTC)

Price at time of writing: $58.82 USD

Founded in 1968 and currently residing in Santa Clara, CA, Intel is the number two (2nd only to Samsung) provider of semiconductors and wireless communications infrastructure and product components.

Current sales stand at $70 billion per year and climbing as a major provider of these services to large companies and government entities.

It maintains low risk with very little competition in the area and is poised for a bright future in the industry. Its strong relationship with many large companies and its cutting edge research to improve its communication system are key to keeping it strong.

It is a great investment for any investor!

Corning (NASDAQ: GLW)

Price at time of writing: $34.46 USD

Founded in 1852 and currently residing in Corning, NY, Corning is a provider of glass, ceramic, and wireless optics.

Current sales stand at $11 billion per year and climbing as the premier provider of these services to major companies and government entities.

It maintains low risk with very little competition in the area and is poised for a bright future in the industry. Its strong relationship with many large companies and its cutting edge research to improve its communication system are key to keeping it strong.

It is a great investment for any investor.

Comcast (NASDAQ: CMCSA)

Price at time of writing: $41.88 USD

Founded in 1953 and currently residing in Philadelphia, PA, Comcast is a provider of broadcasting, telecommunications, and streaming technologies. It is the result of a merger of several companies including NBC, Comcast, and a division of Verizon. Some of its holdings are cable powerhouses such as Syfy and Bravo, as well as the streaming giant HULU.

Current sales stand at $94 billion per year and climbing as the premier provider of these services to major companies and government entities. Its revenue has grown year after year, as shown in the recent sales chart on their website.

It maintains low risk with very little competition in the area and is poised for a bright future in the industry. Its strong relationship with many large companies and its cutting edge research to improve its communication system are key to keeping it strong.

Dell (NASDAQ: DELL)

Price at time of writing: $66.02 USD

Founded in 1984 and currently residing in Round Rock, TX, Dell is a provider of computers, parts, and wireless devices. It has made a name for itself with new innovations in logistics and supply chain operation.

Current sales stand at $78 billion per year and climbing as a premier provider of these products to individuals, major companies, and government entities.

It maintains average risk with the competition in the area and is poised for a bright future in the industry. Its strong relationship with many large companies, brand loyalty, and its cutting edge research to improve its products are a huge pro.

Chapter Seven Growth Stocks Part 4

Cloudera (NASDAQ: CLDR)

Price at time of writing: $10.91 USD

Founded in 2002 and currently residing in Palo Alto, CA, Cloudera is a provider of a software platform for data engineering, data warehousing, machine learning and analytics that runs in the cloud or on premises. Basically, it is a cloud computing repository provider.

Current sales stand at $650 million per year and climbing as a premier provider of these services to major companies and government entities.

It maintains low risk with very little competition in the area and is poised for a bright future in the industry. Its strong relationship with many large companies and its cutting edge research to improve its infrastructure are key to keeping it strong.

It is a strong investment for any investor of any level.

Equinix (NASDAQ: EQIX)

Price at time of writing: $452.50 USD

Founded in 1998 and currently residing in Redwood, CA, Equinix is a provider of internet connection and data centers.

Current sales stand at $4.5 billion per year and climbing as a rising provider of these services to major companies and government entities.

It is average to low risk with some competition in the area and is poised for a bright future in the industry. Its strong relationship with many large companies and its cutting edge research to improve its infrastructure are key to keeping it strong.

It is a very strong stock for those that can afford the purchase price.

FireEye (NASDAQ: FEYE)

Price at time of writing: $15.83 USD

Founded in 2004 and currently residing in Mittapis, CA, FireEye is a provider of cybersecurity and antivirus protection systems.

Current sales stand at $880 million per year and climbing as the premier provider of these services to major companies and government entities.

It maintains low risk with very little competition in the area and is poised for a bright future in the industry. Its strong relationship with many large companies and its cutting edge research to improve its communication system are key to keeping it strong.

It is a very strong stock for any investor at a very affordable price.

Intuit (NASDAQ: INTU)

Price at time of writing: $264.87 USD

Founded in 1983 and currently residing in Mountain View, CA, Intuit is a provider of web-based accounting, tax preparation, and bookkeeping under the brands TurboTax, Quickbooks, Mintm, and Proconnect.

Current sales stand at $5 billion per year and climbing as the premier provider of these services to individuals, major companies, and government entities. Its recent history of income was published on its website and shows consistent growth over time.

It maintains low risk with very little competition in the area and is poised for a bright future in the industry. Its strong relationship with many large companies and its cutting edge research to improve its delivery and pricing are key to keeping it strong.

Veeva Systems (NASDAQ: VEEV)

Price at time of writing: $137.37 USD

Founded in 2007 and currently residing in Pleasanton, CA, Veeva Systems is a provider of cloud-based and content management services.

Current sales stand at $65 billion per year and climbing as the premier provider of these services to major companies and government entities.

It maintains low risk despite competition in the area and is poised for a bright future in the industry. Its strong relationship with many large companies and its cutting edge research to improve its platforms are key to keeping it strong.

It is a strong stock for any investor.

Trade Desk (NASDAQ: TTD)

Price at time of writing: $208.27 USD

Founded in 2009 and currently residing in Ventura, CA, Trade Desk is a provider of web-based investing and brokerage services. It is one of the leaders in the direct investment sector that allows for instant purchases across several exchanges.

Current sales stand at $477 million per year and climbing as the premier provider of these services worldwide. Its recent financials as published on their investor relations page have shown excellent growth, indicating a strong position in the industry.

It maintains a low risk with very little new competition in the area and is poised for a bright future in the industry. Its strong relationships with the exchanges/customers and its cutting edge research to improve its communication system are key to keeping it strong.

Altogether this makes it a great stock for any investor.

Iron Mountain (NASDAQ: IRM)

Price at time of writing: $35.84 USD

Founded in 1951 and currently residing in Boston, MA, Iron Mountain is a provider of web-based and software-based enterprise information and data management.

Current sales stand at $3.5 billion per year and climbing as the premier provider of these services to major companies and government entities.

It maintains low risk with very little competition in the area and is poised for a bright future in the industry. Its strong relationship with many large companies and its cutting edge research to improve its communication system are key to keeping it strong.

It is a good stock for any level of investor.

IBM (NASDAQ: IBM)

Price at time of writing: $140.05 USD

Founded in 1911 and currently residing in Armont, NY, IBM initially started as a provider of office machines and later computers. Today it provides a plethora of computers, software, components, and wireless products to businesses, government, and individuals. It makes up one of the core companies of the DOW Jones Average.

Current sales stand at $79 billion per year and climbing as the premier provider of these services to major companies and government entities. IBM has battled back from recession losses to be sitting as a stable stock. The published earnings report on the IBM website shows excellent stability and growth in recent years.

It maintains low risk despite the competition in the area and is poised for a bright future in the industry. Its strong relationship with many large companies and its cutting edge research to improve its communication system are key to keeping it strong.

A very stable stock for any level of investor.

Taiwan Semiconductor (NASDAQ: TSM)

Price at time of writing: $45.41 USD

Founded in 1987 and currently residing in Taiwan, Taiwan Semiconductor is a provider of semiconductors and wireless infrastructure components.

Current sales stand at $15 billion per year and climbing as an on the rise provider of these products to major companies and government entities.

It maintains low risk despite the competition in the area and is poised for a bright future in the industry especially in the emerging Far East market. Its strong relationship with many large companies and its cutting edge research to improve its products will keep it strong.

A good investment for any investor not afraid of the emerging world.

Thermo Fisher Scientific (NASDAQ: TMO)

Price at time of writing: $263.95 USD

Founded in 2006 and currently residing in San Francisco, CA, Thermo Fisher Scientific resulted from a merger of Thermo Electron and Fisher Scientific. It is a provider of genetic research and micro-precision lab and medical equipment. It owns and supplies under many different brands including Thermo Scientific, Applied Biosystems, and Invitrogen.

Current sales stand at $20 billion per year and climbing as the premier provider of these services to major companies and government entities.

It maintains low risk with very little competition in the area and is poised for a bright future in the industry. Its strong relationship with many large companies and its cutting edge research to improve its systems are key to keeping it strong.

A wise investment for any level of investor.

Exact Sciences (NASDAQ: EXAS)

Price at time of writing: $95.46 USD

Founded in 1995 and currently residing in Madison, WI, Exact Sciences is a lab that concentrates on genetic and microbial research for the purpose of mapping risk down to the atom. It has an exclusive relationship with FDA and conducts a lot of trials for them.

Current sales stand at $6 billion per year and climbing as the premier provider of these services to major companies and government entities.

It maintains low risk with very little competition in the area and is poised for a bright future in the industry. Its strong relationship with many large companies and its cutting edge research to improve its communication system are key to keeping it strong.

A very economical and wise choice for any investor.

Myriad Genetics (NASDAQ: MYGN)

Price at time of writing: $32.24 USD

Founded in 1991 and currently residing in Salt Lake City, UT, Myriad Genetics is a provider of multiple types of genetic testing and other diagnostic products based on molecular biology. Its flagship product is Prolaris, which can map the risk of colon cancer and has extended the lives of many patients.

Current sales stand at $26 billion per year and climbing as the premier provider of these services to major companies and government entities.

It maintains low risk with very little competition in the area and is poised for a bright future in the industry. Its strong relationship with many large companies and its cutting edge research to improve its communication system are key to keeping it strong.

A very economical and wise choice for any investor.

NeoGenomics (NASDAQ: NEO)

Price at time of writing: $19.88 USD

Founded in 2002 and currently residing in Fort Myers, FL, NeoGenomics is a lab that concentrates on genetic and microbial research for the purpose of treating cancer.

Current sales stand at $10 billion per year and climbing as the premier provider of these services to major companies and government entities.

It maintains low risk with very little competition in the area and is poised for a bright future in the industry. Its strong relationship with many large companies and its cutting edge research to improve its communication system are key to keeping it strong.

A very economical and wise choice for any investor.

Nvidia (NASDAQ: NVDA)

Price at time of writing: $191.88 USD

Founded in 1992 and currently residing in Santa Clara, CA, Nvidia is a provider of platforms for gaming, data centers, auto, pro visualization, and now AI. It has garnered a following for its gaming CPUs. Per its website, it does business with the brands GeForce, Quadro, Tegra, and Tesla.

Current sales stand at $9 billion per year and climbing as the premier provider of these services to major companies and government entities.

It maintains low risk with very little competition in the area and is poised for a bright future in the industry. Its strong relationship with many large companies and its cutting edge research to improve its products are key to keeping it strong.

It is a very wise stock for any level of investor.

Micron Technology (NASDAQ: MU)

Price at time of writing: $43.20 USD

Founded in 1978 and currently residing in Boise, ID, Micron Technology is holding and parent company to many subsidiaries that produce computers and semiconductors, and wireless products.

Current sales stand at $20 billion per year and climbing as the premier provider of these services to major companies and government entities.

It maintains low risk with very little competition in the area and is poised for a bright future in the industry. Its strong relationship with many large companies and its cutting edge research to improve its technology system are key to keeping it strong.

Ross (NASDAQ: ROST)

Price at time of writing: $98.65 USD

Founded in 1982 and currently residing in Dublin, CA, Ross is a provider of name brand clothing for men, women, and children and consumer products in a secondary setting. It buys closeouts and overstocks and resells them at over 1000 stores across the Midwest and Northeast.

Current sales stand at $12 billion per year and climbing as the premier provider of these products at low prices. This type of store remains stable in a recession as discounting is big.

It maintains low risk with very little competition in the area and is poised for a bright future in the industry. Its great relationship with retailers and brand awareness is keeping it strong.

A recession proof stock which should hold strong in the coming 36 months.

Amgen (NASDAQ: AMGN)

Price at time of writing: $179.20 USD

Founded in 1980 and currently residing in Thousand Oaks, CA, Amgen works in the pharma industry related to preventing infection in chemotherapy patients and blocking betta transmitters in cancer cells.

Current sales stand at $23 billion per year and climbing as the premier provider of these services to medical providers and researchers.

It maintains low risk with very little competition in the area and is poised for a bright future in the industry. Its strong relationship with many large companies and its cutting edge research to improve its products is key to keeping it strong.

A high potential stock for any investor level.

Dollar Tree (NASDAQ: DLTR)

Price at time of writing: $109.85 USD

Founded in 1986 and currently residing in Norfolk, VA, Dollar Tree is a retailer of low-cost items, food, and consumer products under the Names Dollar Tree and Family Dollar across North America.

Current sales stand at $22 billion per year and climbing as the premier provider of discount items.

It maintains low risk with very little competition in the area and is poised for a bright future in the industry. Its strong relationship with many large companies and its cutting its many locations make it a primary stock and poised for success.

Like Ross, a good solid recession-proof stock for any investor.

Concho Resources (NASDAQ: CXO)

Price at time of writing: $128.31 USD

Founded in 2004 and currently residing in Midland, TX, Concho Resources is a provider of research into bio-carbon and alternative energies. Its vast petroleum holdings make it very successful.

Current sales stand at $4 billion per year and climbing as the premier provider of these services to major companies and government entities.

It maintains low risk with very little competition in the area and is poised for a bright future in the industry. Its strong relationship with many large companies and its cutting edge research to improve its energy offerings/green energy in general are key to keeping it strong.

Great for any investor, especially those interested in green energy.

Nutanix (NASDAQ: NTNX)

Price at time of writing: $43.02 USD

Founded in 2009 and currently residing in India, Nutanix is a provider of web-based cloud business solutions for hyper-converged infrastructure (HCI) appliances and software-defined storage.

Current sales stand at $700 million per year and climbing as the premier provider of these services to major companies and government entities in the Far and Middle East.

It maintains low risk with very little competition in the area and is poised for a bright future in the industry. Its strong relationship with many large companies and its cutting edge research to improve its communication system are key to keeping it strong.

A good investment for those not afraid of investing in the Middle East.

Dropbox (NASDAQ: DBX)

Price at time of writing: $23.42 USD

Founded in 2007 and currently residing in San Francisco, CA, Dropbox is a provider of online file sharing platforms in 17 languages that allow syncing and easy sharing of projects with people all over the world. It offers several levels of service each with different abilities and functions.

Current sales stand at $20 billion per year and climbing as the premier provider of these services to individuals, colleges/schools major companies and government entities.

It maintains low risk with very little competition in the area and is poised for a bright future in the industry. Its strong relationship with many large companies and its cutting edge research to improve its communication system are key to keeping it strong.

Competition from Google will be tough, but the market is big enough for both to co-exist.

Boingo Wireless (NASDAQ: WIFI)

Price at time of writing: $23.68 USD

Founded in 2001 and currently residing in Los Angeles, CA, Boingo Wireless is a provider of wireless internet service to enabled devices with over 1,000,000 wireless networks to use. It is an alternative to the major carriers and data services. It operates and sells a variety of products/services such as traditional wireless and broadband.

Current sales stand at $250 million per year and climbing as the premier provider of these services to major companies and government entities. Including various airports and transportation hubs.

It maintains low risk with very little competition in the area and is poised for a bright future in the industry. Its strong relationship with many large companies and its cutting edge research to improve its communication system are key to keeping it strong.

Genius Brands International (NASDAQ: GNUS)

Price at time of writing: $2.00 USD

Founded in 2013 and currently residing in Los Angeles, CA, Genius Brands International is an entertainment and animation company (formerly DIC) that formed as the result of multiple mergers. It is rebuilding its business and venturing into CGI. This is definitely a company to watch for the future.

Current sales stand at $300 million per year and climbing as it will be a premiere animation company going forward.

It maintains low risk despite the competition in the area due to its strong branding and its past favorites such as Inspector Gadget and Dennis the Menace.

With a industry-wide trend towards tried and true franchises, Genius Brands is poised to be on the up and up over the next few years.

Eastman Kodak (NASDAQ: KODK)

Price at time of writing: $2.46 USD

Founded in 1888 and currently residing in Rochester, NY, Eastman Kodak is a provider of various graphics and art products, software, and devices. It was once the leader in film and photography and invented the digital camera. It has struggled to make a comeback but is poised to reenter the market with its new medical imaging products as well.

It maintains low risk despite the competition in the area and is poised for a bright future in the industry. Its strong relationship with many large companies and its cutting edge research to improve its products, as well as its brand recognition are key to keeping it strong.

This one could go either way, but the medical imaging market potential makes it a solid play for any investor that is willing to buy and hold for an extended time.

Arcimoto (NASDAQ: FUV)

Price at time of writing: $4.00 USD

Founded in 2007 and currently residing in Eugene, OR, Arcimoto is a provider of electric motorized transportation, including tandem two and three wheel bikes. Poised in an industry that is erupting as people move away from cars, Arcimoto is poised to be a leader.

Current sales stand at $650 million per year and climbing as the premier provider of these products to the public.

It maintains low risk with very little competition in the area and is poised for a bright future in the industry. As the industry of green transportation grows so will it.

A great and cheap option for those willing to buy and hold for many years.

Conclusion

Investing your money in the stock market (or anywhere else!) can be overwhelming, but it doesn't have to be.

I hope this information has been beneficial to you and has given you a foundation to invest some of the more unknown companies. There has never been a more exciting time for the market than right now. Even if you feel like you missed the boat with the Apples and Amazons of the world, don't worry, it's never too to get your piece of the pie.

Using dollar cost averaging and putting money into the market each month is a great way to invest. It helps make your investing automatic and allows you to smooth out your investments into a market that moves up and down in an unpredictable way.

Remember to do additional research outside of what you've learned in this book. And for your own sanity, don't check your investments on a daily basis.

Growth stocks in particular can be a volatile market, and you have to be willing to accept that if you are to make long term profits. Perhaps most importantly, don't panic sell if you see a dip in the market.

I wish you the best of luck in the cryptocurrency market, and I hope you make a lot of money.

Finally, if this book has proved useful to you, I'd appreciate it if you took 2 minutes to leave it a review on Amazon.

Made in the USA
Columbia, SC
22 December 2019